Christopher Hervey

Letters from Portugal, Spain, Italy and Germany, in the Years 1759, 1760, and 1761

Vol. 1

Christopher Hervey

Letters from Portugal, Spain, Italy and Germany, in the Years 1759, 1760, and 1761
Vol. 1

ISBN/EAN: 9783337245597

Printed in Europe, USA, Canada, Australia, Japan

Cover: Foto ©ninafisch / pixelio.de

More available books at **www.hansebooks.com**

LETTERS

BY

C. HERVEY, Esq.

FROM

PORTUGAL, SPAIN,

ITALY AND GERMANY,

IN THE YEARS 1759, 1760, AND 1761.

By CHRISTOPHER HERVEY, Esq.

VOLUME THE FIRST.

LONDON:
PRINTED BY J. DAVIS, CHANCERY-LANE; FOR
R. FAULDER, NEW-BOND-STREET.
M.DCC.LXXXV.

LETTERS

FROM

PORTUGAL, &c.

LETTER I.

FALMOUTH, DEC. 20, 1759.

DEAR SIR,

You are to confider this as my firſt and introductory letter to the ſtrict correſpondence you have deſired. The writing ſo much is no trouble, for as I ſhall do it without confidering what I write, I do it likewiſe without difficulty.

You know already that the papers I am to send you are to be upon any subject, as it is the liberty you allow in writing, that makes them no trouble. You are to consider these productions as a strange mixture of incoherences; among which, however, you may chance to find some little matter that suits your taste. All I engage for, is to daub a sheet of paper over with a black fluid called ink; reducing it into certain hieroglyphical characters called letters; which letters shall be put together into little packets called words; and this is all I promise: reserving to myself the full and absolute power of writing in what language or style I please; intelligible or not; good, bad, or indifferent. In consequence of this agreement, you may expect to hear from me next week, and so on, if I am well, till my return to England.

LETTER II.

ON BOARD THE EXPEDITION PACKET,
DEC. 30, 1758.

I HAVE now pretty nearly finished my voyage from Falmouth to Lisbon; and, as I have almost overcome all sea sickness, will give you the paper now due.

On Sunday last, the day before Christmas day, about three o'clock in the afternoon I embarked for Lisbon. I thought, indeed, I should have been left behind; for I had hardly finished dinner, when word was brought that the ship had weighed anchor and was under sail.

By making, however, the boatmen row stoutly, we got up with our packet before she was out of the harbour. Indeed, as it happened, there was no danger of our being left behind, for the Captain of the ship was still on board, and she could not go out to sea till he was set on shore. To explain this seeming paradox you must know, that the Captains of these packets have sometimes the indolent desire of remaining by a comfortable fire-side, while their vessels, under the command of masters, buffet the relentless waves. Their interest likewise in this respect, if I am not misinformed, coincides with their inclinations, as they find it, I believe, turn to better account to act at home as merchants than abroad as sailors. Our sails being at length unfurled, we glided out of Falmouth harbour, with two vessels in our company; the one bound to the Groyne, as we unaccountably call Corunna, and the other to New York. After the second day, indeed, they left us to pursue their respective destinations; while we bore on, in a strait line to the south-west. Our cabin was

crouded

crouded with paffengers, accumulated by a delay of five weeks at Falmouth; there being no packet there but one, which the cuftom-houfe officers had, to our confufion, feized, upon account of her having fome counterband goods on board. Since we embarked, our time has been almoft wholly paft in eating, drinking, and fleep: though, inftead of the latter, I rather ought to fubftitute the bed; which though I have preffed for ten hours every night, but a fmall part of that time was given to repofe. Sometimes, indeed, ftifled with our crouded fituation, I have got upon deck, and taken an evening's walk there, to contemplate that great extent of ocean now fpread all round me. Nothing to engage my eye but the expanfe of the heavens and water; on which latter the veffel I am now failing in rides but as a nut-fhell.

Aut æs aut robur, &c. which I will give in Francis's tranflation of Horace.

> Or oak, or brafs, with triple fold
> That hardy mortal's daring breaft enroll'd,
> Who, firft to the wild ocean's rage
> Launch'd the frail bark, and heard the billows wage
> Impetuous war.

But, formidable as the watery element is, our ifland owes its greatnefs to her being furrounded with it.

> L'orribil mar coll' onda fua vorace
> Forma vallo ficuro all' Anglia audace.

Or, as I fhall attempt to tranflate it in Englifh.

> Old ocean's wave, tho' vex'd with angry ftorms,
> A rampart fure to hardy England forms.

Commerce, likewife, with her hundred joyful attendants, renders this fituation of ours beneficial, even to our enemies; and, had not the old Roman idolatry given place to a much better religion, we ought to inftitute rights in honour of Neptune, as the tutelary deity of England.

LETTER III.

LISBON, DEC. 31, 1758.

I AM arrived fafe in this harbour, but fhall continue on board till I have received an anfwer to a letter I have fent into the town. Our paffage was completed in exactly feven days; for the time they moored at Lifbon this Sunday, was, I believe, the very fame with that in which they had weighed anchor from Falmouth the Sunday before. We were one day becalmed in our voyage; but the others made amends; for it blew fo brifk, that we outrun the mafter's reckoning, and had got to the fouthward of Cape Finifterre, before he imagined we were come into the latitude of it. We did not, however, make land any where thereabout. Indeed, we purpofely kept twenty or thirty leagues off, as the ufual and more fafe navigation.

gation. Had we been nigher within shore, we might have been in danger; for I remember asking the master in the morning where he thought we were, and he told me still in the bay of Biscay, as he knew it by the tumbling sea. But at twelve o'clock, when we made our observations, the Sun still mounted, and we found ourselves two degrees below Cape Finisterre, before we thought we had got into the latitude of it. A proof how very quick our vessel sailed. We should have been at Lisbon a day sooner, but yesterday we could not make land before it was dark, tho' we stood stretching our eyes upon deck, in expectation of seeing it. The Eastern horizon was skirted with a mist, which, I verily believe, was the coast of Portugal; but the Sun's speedy descent hindered our ascertaining it; and we put out to sea for more security. The sky too lowered upon us, and seemed to threaten a south west wind, which is dangerous in these parts. Nor did our master seem entirely at ease.

eafe. He faid, in England a cloudy fky portended nothing; but in thefe countries, where the heavens are generally clear to the higheft degree, a gloomy hemifphere was often the forerunner of bad weather. But his apprehenfions proved groundlefs, and the redoubted fouth-wefter flept peacefully in his cavern. Not that I fpent the night agreeably; on the contrary, it was the worft of all; for the lying to with a high fea communicated a motion to the fhip, by no means agreeable to a landman. The next morning, however, difpelled our fears by a fine diftant profpect of the rock of Lifbon, with the Sun rifing in all his glory behind it. As the land we had made was high ground, and we, confequently, faw it at a great diftance (I believe about twenty leagues off); you will not be furprifed that, tho' we diftinguifhed it at fun-rife, it was a long time before our veffel came up to it. But, imagine a gentle wind had now wafted us clofe to the rock, and that we were juft entering into the mouth

of

of the Tagus. We here obferved a fhip feeming to lie in wait for us at the entrance. It alarmed us at firft, as we thought fhe might be French, and were accordingly in no fmall hurry and confufion, preparing for an engagement. We difcovered, however, at laft, that it was the Hanover packet, juft failed from Lifbon. We hailed each other, fhortened fail, and with great dexterity each fhip went round the other, to know what news. We, indeed, had nothing material. But they informed us, that many of the principal nobles of Portugal had been taken up and thrown into prifon, for the attack upon the king, and that the prefent critical fituation of the affairs of that kingdom had caufed the government to lay an embargo upon the fhipping, which fome Englifh veffels had with difficulty got taken off from them alone. But it is now time for me to lay down the pen, tho' with a *promife of continuation.*

LETTER IV.

LISBON, JAN. 16, 1759.

AFTER we had drained the Hanover packet of all her news, we took leave of her, and each veſſel ſteered their reſpective courſe. We had not proceeded far when a curious ſort of boat came alongſide us, juſt after we had entered the mouth of the Tagus. She was come with a pilot to conduct us into the harbour, as the laws of this country oblige the moſt knowing mariners to have one. This pilot was the firſt Portugueſe I had ever ſeen, which made his appearance the greater entertainment. He had on his long cloak thrown a ſecond time over his left ſhoulder, which, added to a large perpendiculary cocked hat, and a pair of Falſtaff's boots, rendered him altogether a humorous *caricatura*. With much state did he parade up and down the deck, eating salt meat given him by the sailors, who were offended at his paring off the fat and throwing it into the sea, which caused execrations against his *Portuguese stomach*.

In the mean time the ship glided on under his direction, and after having left Cintra, and Mafra, a royal convent, upon the left hand, passed the bar, which is sometimes reckoned dangerous. We know little of bars in England, but the Western rivers of Spain, Portugal, and Barbary, mostly have them, caused, I suppose, by their lying more open to the Atlantic ocean, which drives up heaps of sand into the mouth of them.

We now saw Calcavelas and Cascais, and at last reached Bellem, or, as we pronounce it Bellisle, and the other pretty places situated upon the left hand shore of the river Tagus; all which were less damaged by the earth-

earthquake than the buildings in the centre of the city of Lisbon. Upon a rising ground the king has built a temporary palace, which looks something like a prodigious long stable building, at least from the water, as you see nothing but a low wood-built house, with an extensive row of windows. We, in the mean time, continued our gentle course up the river, and now the city and all the shipping appeared in view. This I think one of the most delightful sights I ever beheld. The *golden* Tagus crouded with vessels of all sorts, and bounded by pretty rising lands on each side, which on the left were covered with houses, formed a most enchanting prospect. As the wind was not over fair, we spent much time in getting to our moorings; but at last our sails were furled, and we accomplished our voyage.

The next morning I went on shore, and a two wheeled chaise, a vehicle used in Lisbon instead of coaches, conducted me to my friend's friend's houfe. I had fcarcely proceeded an hundred yards before the devaftation caufed by the late earthquake prefented itfelf to my view. Heaps of ruins lay on all fides, or where a few houfes remained, they were fo propped up with large pieces of timber, that they rather added to the horror of the fcene. Melancholy reflections occupied me, and I confidered that under my feet might lie hundreds of carcafes, fome of which, by the houfes falling hollow upon them, were deftroyed by the flow-confuming hand of famine, as the fire fubfequent to the earthquake might not reach thefe now fubterraneous regions. In the mean time our chaife continued its progrefs over the rubbifh. They have, indeed, through moft of the ftreets levelled a paffage over the confufed materials of the overthrown buildings. The bookkeeper who attended me caufed me at length to obferve a perfpective view of ruins, through which we were then paffing, and told me, that was once the moft populous

lous ſtreet in Liſbon. Think how affected I muſt be in beholding it a maſs of broken walls, with open windows, through two or three rows of which you diſcovered ſtill farther ruins; a harbour for thieves, owls and goats; in ſhort, the ſeat of deſolation!

After a long ride of four miles, for ſo far did this ſtraggling town extend, we arrived at St. Apollonia, the quarter where my friend dwelt. Liſbon, perhaps, covers as much ground as any city in Europe; but the temporary houſes built in the ſuburbs ſince the earthquake have encreaſed it.

We now, however, talk no more of this calamity. The tumults in which the ſtate is at preſent involved eclipſe, if I may be allowed the expreſſion, their former misfortune, and will probably render me ſpectator of many a melancholy ſcene. It is ſaid the nobles concerned in the nocturnal attack upon the king will be executed in a few days. As
moſt

moſt of them bore a fair character, and are names known in the triumphant days of Portugal, we cannot help dropping a tear of compaſſion for their fate. Pity, however, apart, I enjoy the utmoſt tranquillity in the midſt of this general confuſion. I ſee the lightning blaze round me, but its bolts reach not my humble ſituation.

LETTER V.

LISBON, JAN. 14, 1759.

THE flower of the nobility was executed yesterday. The marchioness of Tavora, a lady who seems to have been generally esteemed, died first. She was beheaded. Her husband and two sons, together with the duke of Aveiro, and the Conde d' Atouguia, were broken upon the wheel, and an assassin last of all burnt alive. All the dead bodies that had been previously executed were consumed along with him, and their ashes swept into the Tagus. Still more they say are to die; but who or when God knows. Some people tell me there is to be another execution in a few days. You see how mysterious every thing is here; but such is the government of Portugal. You shall have hereafter a fuller account of the whole affair, when I can get it with more authenticity; and in the mean time I will give you a defcription of the earthquake, as related by every perfon in this city.

This fatal calamity happened on the firft of November, 1755, between nine and ten o'clock in the forenoon. The weather was ferene the preceding part of the morning, and the fea perfectly calm, when all on a fudden a noife was heard like a rumbling under ground, which continued for fome time, till at laft the fhocks began. In a very fhort fpace they were feveral times repeated, and the ground was feen to move up and down, or tofs to and fro like a fhip at fea. The motion at firft was not fo violent, but as it increafed by degrees, the floors and ceilings began to crack; the roofs to fall, and the arches to give way. From the ruins a prodigious cloud of duft immediately arofe, which overwhelmed the city with fudden darknefs, but which gradually fubfiding, the
trembling

trembling inhabitants of Lisbon re-beheld the Sun. Mr. Woodward, the master of the packet that brought me to Lisbon, was in his ship in the harbour at that time, and the following is his account of the effect of the earthquake upon the water. The first thing he perceived was the noise, which he thought resembled mostly that of another ship running foul of his. He started from his cabin, but when he was upon deck saw no vessel near him. His doubts, however, were soon cleared by a view of the town, which was now rocking; and in a short space afterwards he saw the steeples and towers give way, and fall. Nor was his ship exempt from the agitations experienced upon the land. She at first seemed only to tremble violently, but was afterwards moved perpendicularly up and down upon the water. However, neither Mr. Woodward's nor any other vessel received any considerable damage from the shocks. A great many, indeed, broke their cables and were driven out to sea, for the prodigious strength of the tide was very remarkable, which changed often from ebb to flow, and ran up an down with inconceivable fury. Nothing could equal in the mean time the confusion of the inhabitants of Lisbon. Some fled to the churches, others from the churches to their abandoned houses, and each seemed to imagine the present place the most dangerous. Some were heard to lament their deceased relations; others were seeking them in vain: all joined in lifting up their suppliant hands to heaven, and begging mercy of the incensed deity. Many thought that the day of judgment was approaching; others that it was already come; nor were there wanting those who were afraid that the earth would gape and swallow up at once the city with its inhabitants; for, as every wall was nodding, and a hideous sound proceeded from the bowels of the earth, Lisbon did not only seem to be shaken, but torn from her foundations. At last the ground ceased to move, and the dust in time was

diffi-

dissipated by the wind. But the restored view of Lisbon increased the horror of the scene. That once so populous and flourishing city was now, as every inhabitant imagined, no more. The houses, streets and alleys were strewn with dead bodies. Some had their brains dashed out by the falling of walls and arches, but the greatest part that perished were those who were suffocated by the weight of the rubbish. They dug out a few indeed alive; some after four days, some after six, and some after eight; nor is it a little astonishing they should survive so long. The Roman catholics bring an instance of this in the person of Dionysia Rosa Maria, a girl of fifteen years of age, who they say is now living and well. Though the case may not be authentic in every circumstance, I will relate it. When first the buildings began to shake, she took fast hold of an image of St. Anthony of Lisbon, which she had in her chamber. The house tumbling soon after, she came down along with it, it, mixed and confused in the ruins. Here she lay buried for the space of eight days, without food, till she was found among the dead bodies, and taken out without the least hurt in the presence of John Mello Sampayo, prelate of the holy patriarchal church. In amends for this uncertain account, I will give you another you may depend on, which is the escape of Sir Harry Frankland, the British consul. At the time of the earthquake he was going along the town in his chaise. The noise was the first thing he perceived, as indeed, it was with every person. But he imagined, like the rest, that it was only the King's coach, which generally drives very fast. The shocks, however, that immediately succeeded, soon convinced him what it was. He jumped, therefore, out of his chaise, and ran under the gateway of a house, thinking it was safer than to remain in a narrow street. He had but just taken shelter under the place, when he saw the opposite building fall upon

his

his chaife and fervants, and crufh them to pieces. In about a minute more, the houfe under which he ftood fhared the fame fate. The blows he received from fome falling ftones having ftunned him, he lay for fome time deprived of all fenfation. Upon returning to himfelf, he found the houfe had fallen hollow upon him, though he was confined to fo fmall a compafs as to be able to touch the impending ruins with his hand. What fhocked him moft was, his having fallen upon a woman, who had taken refuge in the fame place, and was now biting his arm in the agonies of death. Having recovered his ftrength a little, he endeavoured to deliver himfelf from this horrid fituation, but fo heavy a ftone lay upon his body, that he could not fhake it off. The ftruggles he made in doing it increafed the woman's agonies, till death, at laft, eafed her of her pain. The conful upon this renewed his efforts, and at laft removed the ftone far enough to be able to crawl from beneath it.

He did not think, however, that his situation was much changed for the better, as the ruins did not permit him to stand up; and he felt besides, that his thigh was considerably bruised, and that he had a couple of wounds in his side. His thigh seemed to have been evidently hurt by the great stone that fell upon it, but he cannot account for his side being wounded in that manner, without it was owing to something he fell against, upon the first crush of the building, before it had beat him quite down to the ground. After he had remained some time in this melancholy situation, he thought he observed at a distance, that a little light glimmered through part of the ruins. Here he immediately crawled in the best manner he was able, and found it to be a small opening between the rubbish. This, by pulling away the stones gently, he gradually enlarged; for no small care was necessary, not to bring the whole upon his head. After much trouble, he worked an opening

large

large enough for his body to pass; but no sooner was he in open air, than the most dismal scene possible was presented to his view. He beheld unhappy Lisbon now laid low in ruins; he heard the shrieks and cries of people buried under them, without being able to give them any assistance; and what made him think his escape more providential was, the fire having arrived to the very street where he then stood, as it was one of the first places in which it got to any head; and by the delay of an hour or two he would have been burnt or smothered. But of this fire (which all say was worse than the earthquake,) I shall speak more fully in my next paper.

LETTER VI.

LISBON, JAN. 20, 1759.

THE wrath of Heaven was not yet fatiated with the overthrow of Lisbon, tho' near half destroyed by the earthquake, and chose to afflict it with a new and still worse disaster. A fire broke out the same day in various parts of the city. This is easily accounted for by the timber and furniture falling upon the fire-places within the houses after they were thrown down. Besides, as it was the anniversary of All Saints, the altars of their churches were adorned with infinite numbers of wax lights. Nor was there help sufficient to check the flames upon their first breaking out, as most of the people had been dispersed about the fields in a state of stupefaction. This gave the fire

fire time to spread on every side, and in four days it consumed more than one half of the private houses, and most of the principal buildings. I will not trouble you with a list of the public edifices that were destroyed. To these we may add the loss of innumerable records, public deeds, bonds, books of merchandize, parish books of baptisms, funerals and genealogies, without which no property can be settled, nor rights of inheritance sufficiently proved. Immense quantities of plate and money was either entirely lost, or melted together in a mass, so as not to be distinguished by the owner. Nor were multitudes of valuable pictures, hangings, pearls, diamonds, and other precious stones, ever recovered. In a word, every thing magnificent and valuable in the city was, for the most part, spoiled or consumed by the devouring flames; and the only way left of determining property or debts, was by the oaths of the parties, which many were wicked enough to turn to their advantage.

Nor

Nor were the earthquake and succeeding fire the only enemies to Lisbon. The incredible rising of the waters bore away a number of people and things. It seems probable that the motion which shook the earth was communicated to the neighbouring seas. Whatever might be the cause, undoubted was the effect; for at Cascais, Setuval, Peniche, and even at Cadiz, many people were drowned by the inundations; and at Lisbon the land was so far overflowed by the waters of the ocean, that bridges were destroyed, walls overturned, and many things of immense weight carried off to sea.

The city being thus destroyed, and the water affording but an inhospitable asylum to boats, the principal hopes remaining to the inhabitants were to fly into the neighbouring fields. Hither they flocked in crouds, uncertain afterwards whither to direct their weary steps. Their flight had been difficult; for the town was encumbered

bered with heaps of ruins, which were often extremely high. In some parts they had been obliged to force away the rubbish with their hands, and creep, or climb, according as occasion offered. Many images of distress might be represented, but I leave your imagination to form a picture of the general horror.

The King and Queen, with the Princess of Brazil, the Infantas her sisters, and the Infant Don Pedro, were at that time by good fortune at their country palace, pleasantly situated three miles out of town towards the west. They got safe into the garden at the beginning of the earthquake, and from thence retired to a neighbouring seat, and erected tents, where they lived some months, till a wooden palace was run up for them. It was built at the same place they were at during the earthquake, by name Bellem, but names do not much signify to you, who were never upon the spot.

In

In my next paper you shall have some account of the people's proceedings, after these extreme calamities.

LETTER VII.

LISBON, JAN. 25, 1759.

THE night fucceeding the earthquake afforded but little reft to the late inhabitants of Lifbon, and that under the open air. The fhocks were frequently repeated, and the whole city lay involved in flames and fmoke. Thofe who, wearied with the fatigue of the day, had funk down overpowered by fleep, were foon awakened by new fhocks and by the cries of the furrounding multitude, imploring the divine mercy, and the interceffion of the faints. Who could have imagined that the inhabitants of fo populous, fo wealthy and luxurious a city, fhould be reduced to fuch a degree of mifery and want, as to have the earth alone for their bed, and the air only for their covering! They, at laft, however, had recourfe

to

to little tents made of blankets and sheets, and afterwards ran up wooden huts, to defend themselves from the inclemency of the weather. Provisions were likewise, at first, so scarce, that those who had nothing but dry bread thought themselves very rich and happy. The King did what he could to assist his subjects upon so melancholy an occasion. He distributed medicines to the sick, and provisions to those who were in health. He furnished several with materials for propping their ruinous buildings, and with money. In this latter respect, the example of the monarch was followed by the princes and princesses of the royal family; and several other lords and private persons. The King made, likewise, various other regulations for the public safety. Among the rest, he ordered that none of the magistrates or nobility should leave Lisbon, and that the price of things should remain the same as before. Persons were likewise sent to the provinces of the kingdom,

dom, to invite those who had fled from the city to return, and use compulsion, if necessary, with the labourers and tradesmen. A number of soldiers were ordered from the different towns of Estremadura and Alentejo, to reinforce the king's troops at Lisbon, where they were employed in assisting the ministers and royal officers in burying the dead; in levelling the streets and highways: and in guarding several places from the attacks of thieves. Of these there was such a number dispersed about the town, that no house was secure from being robbed; no church from being sacrilegiously plundered. Nor were even the bodies of the dead exempt from their violence, as they stripped them of whatever was most valuable. Orders were immediately issued for proceeding with the utmost severity, and without delay, against offenders of that sort. In consequence of which, thirty-four were hanged within the space of a few days, viz. eleven Portuguese, ten Spaniards, five Irishmen,

men, three Savoyards, two Frenchmen, one Polander, one Fleming, and one Moor. The direction of these affairs was committed to the duke de Lafoens, the king's cousin-german, and the first peer in Portugal.

The great shock, which lasted about seven minutes, was followed by four more, which, tho' of shorter duration, were of greater violence. The first of them was at eleven o'clock, a little above an hour after the principal shock. The second was upon the eighth day of the same month of November, before break of day. The third the eleventh of December, also before break of day. The fourth happened the twenty-first of the same month, about nine o'clock in the morning. There has, however, been besides a most amazing number of slighter shocks; and especially for the succeeding six months after the first. The earth too opened in various places, but did not form such caverns as have been represented by some,

some, as the largest crack was hardly able to swallow a man and horse. Some of these kept open for near a fortnight. The waters, likewise, of the wells and springs became of a turbid colour and offensive smell. But one of the most remarkable, as well as most horrid effects of the earthquake, was the disappearance of the key upon the river Tagus, which sunk under water, with above a hundred and fifty people upon it. As the custom-house stood near it, part of that was swallowed up also. The place was, out of curiosity, fathomed a day or two after, but no bottom could be found; and for a long time there remained a considerable depth of water, which, however, at present is reduced to five fathom. It is said that one escaped this horrid death, but I should hardly think it possible for the best swimmer to resist the eddies of water occasioned by the sinking of the key. What number of inhabitants were destroyed upon the whole, in the earthquake, is difficult to tell with any exactnefs. A Portuguefe author thinks we might reckon them at about fifteen thoufand. Some, indeed, pretend that feventy thoufand perifhed, but they do not feem to confider, that the lofs of people was not in proportion to the number of houfes demolifhed. Certain, however, it is, that a great number loft their lives in this unhappy affair, and that Lifbon will, for many years, remember the fatal firft of November, 1755.

LETTER IX.

LISBON, JAN. 30, 1759.

LITTLE or nothing more remains concerning the earthquake worthy your being made acquainted with. What was principally apprehended immediately after it, was the perishing with hunger; but when the space of a day or two had a little quieted the apprehensions of the labouring people, provisions were again brought from the country. The city is said to have made a most horrid appearance by night after it had taken fire. In the day time little more was to be observed at a distance but the smoke. It no sooner however become dark than the flames were visible, shining bright through the windows of the buildings that were still upright. Nor were the ships in the harbour totally secure from the conflagration. The wind

wind blew sparks and lighted pieces of wood upon their decks. Much care was necessary, for the sailors to exempt their vessels from the common fate of Lisbon. It is said, that one was quite set on fire, and having broken from her moorings, was driven up the river by the current all in a blaze. The English factory, after some days, united, and with much difficulty hired a house a few miles out of town, where they lived together a month. This union was the more necessary, as the Roman catholics were, at this time, particularly bigoted; and, consequently, more than ordinarily vehement against the protestants. They proceeded almost by force in making proselytes, and in one case did actually so. A malicious idea had likewise gained some little ground, that heaven had afflicted the city of Lisbon in this manner for suffering so many heretics to dwell in it. And yet the English church was the only one that had remained unhurt under its fury. These ideas,

ideas, added to the fanatic madness of their priests, who ran wildly about the streets, with relics and crucifixes in their hands, crying out repentance and confession, made the English most desirous of collecting themselves into a body, which they did, as I have already mentioned. They never undressed for the first fortnight, and slept in a room all together; lying upon the best materials they could get, and in their chamber hung burning an old lanthorn. Every noise alarmed them, and every motion was an earthquake. In consequence of these agitated imaginations, they were continually hurrying out of doors in great confusion. The gentlemen in the mean time dispatched their servants to Lisbon, to secure the ruins of their houses from being plundered, as they were informed of the great quantity of robbers, notwithstanding the frequent executions of the government. And even these servants were scarcely able to restrain the audaciousness of the rogues, who were hardly driven out

out from one corner, than they returned on the oppofite fide. In a few days each perfon began digging in his refpective ruins, and many things would have been recovered, if the fire had not mixed and deftroyed the whole. Curiofities of this kind were afterwards fold at a high price, as gold and filver run together, and other things of this fort. The merchants, however, fuffered principally by the lofs of their books, as it incapacitated them from claiming debts, which the Portuguefe were unwilling to pay. During this interval of time, the workmen had run up a few flight houfes of wood, which were inhabited for above a year, till better accommodations caufed them to be abandoned. New buildings, however, were not allowed to be raifed within the precincts of the city, as the court had, foon after the earthquake, iffued out an edict to the contrary. The intention of this was to give time to prepare a proper plan for the rebuilding of the town, which, they fay, has

at

at length been given out; but nothing has been put in execution; nor, indeed, has any thing been done since the earthquake, except removing the obstruction of stones and lumber from the streets. The deficiency of money is reported, and with probability, to be the cause of this delay, as the fresh duties laid upon imports and exports for that purpose, are by no means sufficient to answer such expences.

LETTER X.

LISBON, FEB. 3, 1759.

I WILL now attempt to give you some account of the late disturbances that have happened in this kingdom of Portugal. It is not, however, easy to get the certain truth of every thing, upon account of the great secrecy this government observes in all its proceedings.

The Portuguese jesuits considering themselves injured by their being prohibited from preaching and hearing confessions in these dominions, upon account of their conduct in the Brazils, had for some time nourished an inveterate hatred against the king and present government. They had, at last, flattered themselves with being able to revenge

venge their imagined wrongs by ſtirring up
the Tavora family, and ſome other nobles
that were diſaffected to his majeſty, to an
open attempt againſt his life. One of the
principal incitements they made uſe of, was the
unlawful correſpondence ſuppoſed to be carried
on between the king and the young marchio-
neſs of Tavora, wife to the young marquis of
the ſame title, who ſuffered a few days ago.
The jeſuits, and Malagrida, one of them in
particular, did not fail to exaggerate the
heinouſneſs of this crime to the utmoſt of
their power. They repreſented how igno-
minious it was, that a perſon, who had the
honour of being allied by marriage to the
illuſtrious name of Tavora, ſhould become a
proſtitute even to a king. That all his
titles ought not to defend this haughty
violator of the moſt ſacred laws of religion
from their vengeance; that his death was
regiſtered in heaven, and the authors of it
would be guilty only of a *venial ſin,* for
which the cauſe would eaſily atone. In
this

this manner, and by similar expressions, are the jesuits reported to have inflamed the Tavora family to their desired pitch. Nor did they less shew their art, in uniting to their interests a rival of the Tavoras, by name the duke of Aveiro, who, notwithstanding some favours received, had been always a professed enemy to the king and his administration. Things thus prepared, several rumours and prophecies were spread abroad, that the king's life was not of long duration; and some even limited it to the month of September last, on the third day of which the assassination of the king was attempted. The persons concerned in it were the duke of Aveiro, the marquis of Tavora, with his wife, and two sons; the count of Atouguia, his son in law; Joseph Romeiro, a corporal in one of the regiments belonging to the Tavora family, who were all in the army; Emanuel Alvarez Ferreira, Antonio Alvarez Ferreira, and Joseph Policarpio; the first valet de chambre of the duke of Aveiro,

and

and the two others relations of Emanuel Alvarez Ferreira. These, with John Miguel, the duke's footman, completed the number that were to attack the king. They determined to execute their design one night, as his majesty was returning from the young marchioness of Tavora, who was then at her country seat, some few miles out of Lisbon. This was the third of September. Accordingly, the duke of Aveiro, with his footman, John Miguel, posted themselves the first in the road, where the king was to pass, under a sort of arch; which has since, upon that account, been pulled down. Antonio Alvarez Ferreira, and Joseph Policarpio, were stationed a little below them, upon the same road. The duke's piece missed fire, as the king passed in his chaise. The postilion, who observed the sparks struck from the flint, spurred his mules to a full gallop. This rendered the aim of the other two, placed below the duke, very uncertain; but they did, at last, by galloping after the chaise, chaife, fire through the back of it, and wounded the king, though not mortally. He would not, however, have efcaped the remaining parties on the road, placed ftill lower, if he had not ordered his poftilion, upon finding himfelf hurt, to go immediately to his furgeon general's houfe, by which means, as the road luckily turned off at that place, he efcaped their ambufcade.

The king was no fooner paffed, than the feveral parties reunited, uncertain of the effects of their attempt. Some affirmed that the king muft have fallen; others were doubtful of their fuccefs. The next morning they heard the mortifying news of his majefty's being arrived at his palace and wounded only in the arm. Upon this they formed a fort of council of war, at which the old marchionefs of Tavora was prefent, as fhe was at all their meetings. They here agreed upon there being no fear of a difcovery, and that provided they remained true to each other, mortal power could never fathom the secret. But the abilities of the present secretary of state, Sebastian Joseph de Carvalho, thwarted their hopes. Nor was he sorry, I believe, for the present opportunity of cutting off some noblemen, who, envious of so much power being conferred upon a simple gentleman, were continually opposing his advancement. He was formerly envoy from Portugal to the court of England, but recalled, it is said, by desire of our king. The Portuguese are thought to detest him, but suffer in silent indignation the favourite of their sovereign. By his advice the present affair was as much as possible stifled. Reports were immediately issued, that the king had been slightly wounded by robbers, on his return from the country. In the mean time no underhand means were neglected to discover the traitors, which by great art was at last imperfectly done. But when Sebastian Joseph found them of so high rank, not a little ad-

dress

dress seemed still wanting to submit them to his power. He desired his royal master to behave towards them with the usual civility, whilst he collected in and near Lisbon the major part of the forces of the whole kingdom, under pretence of invasions from Spain, and other fictitious tumults. No sooner were they arrived, than guards were sent to the various houses of the criminals, who were all, with the major part of their relations, taken up in little more than the space of one hour. Sebastian Joseph now threw off the mask, and published a manifesto, ordering every person to declare what they knew concerning the present conspiracy, or they would be considered as equally culpable, with the criminals themselves. An embargo was also laid upon the shipping, nor was any person permitted to go out of Lisbon, without a passport. This embargo caused some words between the commanding officer of three English men of war, then in the Tagus, and the secretary of state;

but

but they at length got leave to depart with other English ships. I will conclude, by shewing you a little the style of this country, and sending you a translation of the latter edict, published by Carvalho, forbidding any person's departure from Lisbon without a passport. The former, obliging every Portuguese subject to give in information is much longer, but I may perhaps give it you in my next paper.

" Royal Edict.

" Our sovereign lord the king commands,
" that no person or persons whatsoever, be
" their condition or quality what it may,
" dare to depart from this court, or its ad-
" jacent district, either by sea or land, until
" fresh orders from us, without the said
" person or persons do first appear, and
" justify their departure in the presence of
" Doctor Stephen Peter de Carvalho Di-
" simbargador, inhabiting at Santa Marina;
" and appointed by his majesty to receive

" the

" the said justifications, as also to issue out
" proper passports resulting from them;
" and this under penalty, that the person
" or persons daring to depart without such
" passports, shall be reconducted to Lisbon
" at their own expence, besides being liable
" to due punishment for disobedience to
" the royal command.

" N. B. These passports are only to re-
" main in force for the space of four and
" twenty hours.

" Given at our palace at Bellem, Decem-
" ber 13, 1758.

" (Signed)   *Sebastian Joseph de Carvalho.*"

LETTER XI.

LISBON, FEB. 7, 1759.

THE following is the royal manifesto or edict obliging every Portuguese subject to give due information.

"Although the subjects of Portugal have for many ages been celebrated for the observation of that inviolable attachment due to their kings and natural sovereigns, cultivating with the greatest piety those holy and unalterable obligations; yet have we, notwithstanding, been so unhappy in our days to find, that among the very natives of this kingdom, certain particular persons there are, who, forgetful of those ancient and noble exam-

"ples

" ples, have with infernal idea dared to
" form a moſt ſacrilegious and abominable
" conſpiracy. It began with their ſuggeſt-
" ing and declaring underhand, in order to
" abuſe the ſincerity of thoſe perſons who
" were adorned with more pious inclina-
" tions, that our royal life was not to con-
" tinue long; uttering this in the tone of
" prophecies; nay, even limiting the time
" of our death to the following month of
" September. No ſooner had the ſaid con-
" ſpirators, by ſimilar malicious rumours,
" diſpoſed the minds of the people to their
" deſires, than they proceeded to more atro-
" cious actions; and to verify their predic-
" tions by the never enough to be abhorred
" attack made upon our royal perſon, the
" third of the ſaid month of September.
" We were paſſing, at eleven at night,
" through the little field, * in order to retire

* Called in Portuguese campo pequenho, in oppoſition to campo grande, or the great field, not far from it.

" to

"to our palace, when three of the afore-
"mentioned conspirators lying in wait on
"horseback, in the aforesaid place, under
"cover of the low houses thereunto adjoin-
"ing, did with ever infamous and execrable
"treason, at the back of the chaise in
"which we were sitting, fire three pistols
"or blunderbusses, so deeply charged with
"slugs, that although one missed fire, yet
"the other two were sufficient, not only
"to make two round apertures of enormous
"bigness in the back of the chaise in
"which we were sitting, but even to break
"and tear away every thing they approach-
"ed; so that mortal judgment cannot form
"idea how our royal person, when confined
"within so narrow a compass, could escape
"with only receiving many deep wounds,
"was not the whole to be attributed to that
"omnipotent hand, which by evident mira-
"cles preserved and defended us, amidst
"the ruins and horror of that dreadful
"attack. Now the sacred principles of all

,, laws,

"laws, divine, natural and civil, being
"moſt ſacrilegiouſly offended by this action,
"to the univerſal ſhame of religion and
"humanity; theſe conſiderations render it
"indiſpenſibly neceſſary to avenge this
"crime, eſpecially, as the ſcandal is ſo
"great from thence redounding upon the
"loyalty of the Portugueſe, whoſe excel-
"lent ſentiments of honor, love, and gra-
"titude towards our royal perſon, would
"never permit them to be at eaſe, without
"the moral certainty, that this moſt execra-
"ble conſpiracy was torn up from its very
"roots, ſo as not to leave among our faith-
"ful ſubjects one of thoſe monſters, who
"dared to arrive at ſuch a height of enor-
"mous wickedneſs. We decree, therefore,
"that all thoſe perſons, who ſhall manifeſt
"unto us (provided they prove what they
"declare,) any one or more of the traitors
"concerned in this infamous conſpiracy,
"the ſaid informers ſhall, if plebeians, be
"immediately created gentlemen; if gen-
"tlemen,

"tlemen, shall have our letters patent for
" becoming fidalgo; * or, if fidalgo,
" knight of some order, with all the privi-
" leges thereunto belonging; in fine, be
" their rank what it will, we will grant
" unto them still higher titles and honors,
" over and above all which honors, the
" said informers shall enjoy many pecuniary
" advantages, as well as offices of justice,
" court places, and military preferments:
" reserving to ourself, and to our judgment,
" the regulation of these rewards, accord-
" ing to the nature and importance of the
" service administered. Nor shall the ac-
" complices of this abominable conspiracy,
" so not principally concerned, be exempt
" from the abovementioned favors, besides
" which, upon due confession and informa-
" tion, we here grant them our royal
" pardon. Our magistrates, likewise, who

---

* Or hidalgo in Spanish, is a rank in Spain and Portugal, which answers to that of our noblemens' sons.

" shall

" shall apprehend such criminals, shall
" have new honors and advancements due
" to their services conferred upon them;
" enjoying moreover all the foregoing re-
" wards, in case of their being also in-
" formers; for no person can nor ought to
" conceal malefactors of so high a nature,
" upon the false idea that the character
" of an informer is disreputable. We here
" advertise all our subjects, that reflexions
" like these, though they may take place
" in trivial affairs, are not only not to be
" incurred by discovering actions of con-
" spiracy and of high treason against the
" supreme prince, but, on the contrary,
" those who know any thing of such
" crimes, and do not publish what they
" know in proper time, incur the penalty
" and the same dishonor with those crimi-
" nals who are convicted of such facts.
" Nor are fathers excusable in concealing
" their children, or children their fathers,
" as the prior obligations towards their
" king

"king and country, the common fathers of
"every subject, always prevail before the
"ties of birth; especially in misdemeanors
"of so atrocious a nature, and so prejudi-
"cial to society. And for the easier appre-
"hending of the said criminals, it is our
"royal pleasure, that the power of all our
"magistrates within this kingdom be uni-
"versal, extending itself to every part of
"the kingdom; and all being invested with
"a similar power, so as to be able to act
"from their own authority with regard to
"the speedy apprehending of criminals,
"without waiting for orders from the im-
"mediate magistrates of the crown. Nay,
"suspected persons may even be taken up
"by private men, provided they conduct
"them forthwith to the nearest magistrate,
"who, finding due cause of suspicion, shall
"send them properly secured to this court.
"The Doctor Pedro Gonsalvez Cordeiro
"Pereira of our council, and Disimbargador
"of the palace, shall cause this our decree
"to

" to be affixed in all public places within
" the city of Lisbon, and the districts ad-
" joining; sending copies thereof, signed
" with his name, to all the other towns
" and cities of these kingdoms; and we
" declare, that the said copies shall have
" equal force and authority with their ori-
" ginals, notwithstanding any law, disposi-
" tion, or custom to the contrary, be they
" even among the number of those to dero-
" gate from which requires our express
" command.

" BELLEM, *December* 9, 1758.

" Signed with his majesty's seal."

LETTER XII.

LISBON, FEB. 10, 1759.

THE royal edict of which I gave you a tranflation in my former paper, was, according to the order, hung up in all confpicuous parts of the city, and foon after the Juez del Povo, or, as we might call him, the mayor of Lifbon, prefented the following fupplication to his majefty, through the hands of his fecretary of ftate, to whom it was addreffed.

" The mayor of the city of Lifbon has
" the honor of begging your excellency
" to lay before the royal prefence of his
" majefty, that his moft juft edict was with
" many tears read by all his faithful people
" of Lifbon, all of whom earneftly demand
" juftice

" justice against an attempt so nearly affect-
" ing the loyalty of the Portuguese, and
" for the avenging of which they with
" impatience expect the royal orders. His
" excellency is likewise desired to assure his
" majesty, that it is the most fervent wish
" of his loyal subjects to shed the very last
" drop of their blood in the defence and
" for the glory of their sovereign."

Whilst these edicts and addresses were interchanging, the unhappy criminals were suffering various tortures in their respective prisons. It will be difficult for me to ascertain the names and exact number of the nobility that were now under arrest, and it will be sufficient to tell you, they were esteemed the flower of Portugal. They were all taken up, as I have before remarked, at the same time, and without the least stir made in their defence by the populace, who, though they might have entertained similar inclinations, were rendered incapable of

putting

putting them in execution, by having been deprived of their arms. This was by order of the minifter, and in confequence of it, every houfe had been fearched by foldiers, and all weapons feized, particularly in gun-fmith's fhops, and other places where they were to be found in quantities. Gentlemen, however, and efpecially foreigners, were treated with more civility, and their word of honor that they had no arms was fufficient. They were promifed to be returned in a few days, but I have not yet heard of its being done. As for the government's proceedings againft the principal criminals, during their continuance in prifon, it is difficult to get at the truth of them. Vulgar rumour loads them with chains, and ftretches them upon racks; but I fhould think without better foundation than our natural propenfity to imagine the worft of what we are ignorant. That they fuffered tortures to enforce confeffion is, I believe, true; but I cannot think that human nature

could

could grow so wanton in punishments as common report was represented; nor that the duke of Aveiro was kept perpetually riveted to earth. Some, indeed, who were present at their execution affirmed that they had lost the use of their wrists, which might be true, without such horrid torments being used, as make nature shudder, and imagination fleet with hasty wing to happier climes.

But the government was so mysterious that we were not even certain there was to be an execution till the preceding evening; when the erection of a scaffold sufficiently manifested that some person was to die in the morning; but who were to be the victims remained equally unknown. In the morning of the 13th of January, before break of day, a large body of troops marched to the square of Bellem, the place where they had erected the scaffold. It consisted only of plain boards, not even covered with black cloth, a thing very uncommon when nobles are to die. It was

was done to fhew that they were degraded from their rank by the action they had committed; and for the fame reafon the fervants, &c. were put to death with their mafters. Not long after fun-rife all was in readinefs for the execution, of which I will now give you the beft defcription in my power, from hearfay; as I was not prefent, nor ever will at fcenes of this nature. My ears, however, were unwilling auditors of every minute circumftance, as the world feems to have pleafure in the recital of unfortunate events. The firft conducted upon the fcaffold was the marchionefs of Tavora, a lady who bore a great character in Lifbon for her good nature and gentility. She was beheaded, tho' not with an axe in our manner, but with a kind of long broad knife. She fat, or, I believe, was rather tied to a fort of ftool, from behind which the executioner, with one ftroke, feparated her head from her body. This was the principal of what could be obferved by the fpectators, the neareft of whom
were

were kept off above an hundred yards from the scaffold by the surrounding troops. Some people in ships might, indeed, be nearer, as one side of the square of Bellem is bounded by the Tagus. The knife glittered much, as the sun struck upon it, while the executioner was holding it behind the marchioness of Tavora. She was dead by eight o'clock— but we did not know who was to follow her. There was a report about this time that the guards, who patroled the streets, permitted no person to approach the square of Bellem, but without foundation. No sooner was the marchioness executed, than they placed her corpse upon a sort of bench prepared upon the scaffold. They threw a black cloth over it. Her eldest son at length succeeded his unhappy mother in his death. His fate was more rigorous, as he was broken upon the wheel, or, to speak more properly, upon a sort of St. Andrew's Cross. He was tied to these two pieces of wood, and laid flat upon the ground, after which the executioner,

with

with a large iron crow, formed at the end, in some measure, like a hammer, struck him nine blows, two upon each arm and leg, and one upon the breast, which was imagined to be given first. But for the truth of this we must give credit to the trial, and their sentences, which were published about three days afterwards; as none of the spectators were near enough to distinguish upon what part of the body the blows first fell, tho' most agree that the duke of Aveiro was, undoubtedly, broken alive. In this manner perished the second,—that young lady's husband with whom the king is reported to have had his intrigue. He is said to have been very apprehensive of death, as likewise the duke of Aveiro, whom, indeed, I ought not yet to mention, as he was executed the last but one. The third victim who appeared upon the scaffold, was the younger son of the marchioness of Tavora, who, tho' but a lad of eighteen years old, is said to have behaved the best of all. He knelt for some moments

' F before

before the corpse of his mother, and was afterwards executed in the same manner as his brother. Next came the father, who suffered the same punishment, tho' if we may believe the sentence, the *coup de grace* was given him the very last stroke. The Conde d' Atouguia died next. His lady is reported to have lost her senses, tho' the nuns of the convent where she is confined, had strict orders not to inform her of her unhappy husband's fate. But rumours only of what had happened, together with the complaints of her children, might well be sufficient to turn her brain. All the ladies whose husbands or relations were concerned in this affair are now confined in convents with their families. Each family have a particular monastry allotted them for a prison, without any communication being permitted with the rest. After the execution of the Conde d' Atouguia, Bras Joseph Romeiro, Juan Miguel, and Emanuel Alvarez Ferreira, all of low birth, were broken upon the same kind of

St.

St. Andrew's Crofs. The ninth that fuffered was the duke of Aveiro, who was broken alive. The bodies of the criminals, as foon as they expired, were laid upon an equal number of wheels prepared on pupofe. Thefe mournful inftruments were nailed horizontally upon high poles, and covered with black cloth after their bodies were extended upon them, if I may ufe that expreffion, as one of the objects which principally ftruck the beholders, was the contracted mafs in which they lay. Though the wheels were fmall, their mangled limbs did not reach beyond their circumference; but the black cloth hung perpendicularly down in the circle which they formed. The moft terrible execution now approached, that of Antonio Alvarez Ferreira. He was fentenced to be burnt alive, together with Jofeph Policarpio de Azevedo, the two perfons who had wounded the king. Jofeph Policarpio, however, had found means to fly the kingdom, tho' in what manner is uncertain. Some fay that

that returning on horseback to the duke of Aveiro's, the day that nobleman was arrested, —upon seeing his palace surrounded with guards, he galloped to the out-skirts of the town, and there giving some money to a beggar to exchange clothes, passed in that manner through the Portuguese troops posted round Lisbon. But in whatever manner he escaped, he, undoubtedly, only suffered execution in effigy, whilst his companion, Antonio Alvarez Ferreira, was bound in reality to the stake. They girt him only with a chain about his middle. The fastening it to the stake took up some time, during which he seemed to behave with great resolution, as he did likewise while they were surrounding him with rosin, pitch, tar, and other combustible materials. They laid the same also round the other executed bodies, which were all by the sentence to be reduced to ashes, and thrown into the sea. After these preparations, the mangled carcases of the antecedent sufferers were uncovered, and the poor remaining criminal

minal had the whole melancholy scene displayed to his view. They then set on fire in various parts the entire scaffolding. It is reported, however, that the pitch was so badly laid about the unhappy sufferer, that it was long before the flames, interrupted by a contrary wind, reached him; and that he was seen for some time to wreath about, and even his shrieks were said to have been heard by many. As soon as the pile, bodies and all, were consumed, tho' not so perfectly as they ought to have been; the ashes were carried away in baskets, and thrown into the Tagus, which, perhaps, at Bellem may almost deserve the name of an arm of the sea. After this they covered the place of execution with some new mould, and tho' I was upon the very spot the next morning, I could hardly distinguish any difference between that and the adjacent ground. Thus finished this fatal day, long to be remembered in the annals of Portugal.

LETTER XIII.

LISBON, FEB. 13, 1759.

I WILL now give you a translation of what the court published immediately after the execution you have had so terrible an account of in my foregoing paper. I shall then tell you what we know concerning the jesuits, to all whose convents Sebastian Joseph put a guard of soldiers at the same time that he caused the nobles to be arrested. But what I am going to send a translation of, will take up some room, without I can contrive to abridge it, which I will endeavour to do.

" The council and disimbargador of our
" sovereign lord the king, agree, &c. and
" have, by force of law and decree of his
" majesty, after consulting all depositions,
                                    " papers,

"papers, allegations, articles, and defences
"condemned the following persons; viz.
"Joseph Mascarenias, who was duke of
"Aveiro; Donna Leonoro de Tavora, who
"was marchioness of the same title; Fran-
"cis de Assis de Tavora, who was marquis
"of the same title; Don Lewis Bernar-
"do de Tavora, his son, who was likewise
"marquis of the same title; Don Jerony-
"mo de Ataide, who was count of Atou-
"guia; Joseph Maria de Tavora, aid de
"camp to his father the late marquis; Brass
"Joseph Romeiro, lately corporal of the
"company which belonged to Lewis Ber-
"nardo de Tavora, the criminal; Antonio
"Alvarez Ferreira, Joseph Policarpio de
"Azevedo, Emanuel Alvarez Ferreira, valet
"de chambre to the criminal Joseph Mas-
"carenias, and John Miguel, footman to the
"said criminal.

" For

" For first,

" It is proved, partly by the confession of most of the criminals, and partly by eye witnesses agreeing with the former, that Joseph Mascarenias, late duke of Aveiro, had conceived a mortal hatred against the king, because his majesty had frustrated his designs of getting into his own hands all influence in the government, a thing which he enjoyed in the late reign by means of the Friar Gaspar da Encarnaçaon, his uncle. He had also been hindered by the august and sacred person of our sovereign lord the king from making several chaces and commendaries hereditary in his family, which he was to enjoy only for life, as well as from marrying his son, the marquis of Gouvea, to Donna Margherita de Lorena, next sister and immediate heiress to the present duke of Cadaval; by which marriage he hoped to unite the riches of the house of Cadaval to his own; the present duke not
" having

" having yet had the small pox, which is
" fatal in that family, besides his being a
" minor, and yet unmarried; from enter-
" ing into which marriage state Joseph
" Mascarenias endeavoured to hinder him
" by encouraging law suits against him, in
" order to put his revenues into such con-
" fusion, that he might not be able to bear
" the expences which attend marriage in
" persons of his condition.

" 2dly, It is proved that the said Joseph
" Mascarenias laboured to get into his party
" all malecontents, and other persons that
" were out of favor, and by his calumnies
" and hatred against his majesty still in-
" creased their disaffection; exhorting them
" to fly from and abhor the king's service,
" setting them the example of it, and say-
" ing oftentimes, that when an order came
" for him to go to court, it was the same as
" if an order was sent him to cut off his
" legs; nay, his rash presumption hurried
" him

" him to such lengths, that he flattered
" himself, and with pleasure hearkened to
" people who told him that he had no far-
" ther to rise than to the throne.

" 3dly, It is proved, moreover, that
" whereas the said Joseph Mascarenias had
" always an irreconcileable aversion to
" the jesuits, during the administration of
" his uncle Friar Gaspar da Encarnaçaon,
" and also after his death; yet upon their
" being forbidden the palace for their be-
" haviour in the Indies, he was suddenly
" reconciled to them, visiting them fre-
" quently in all their convents, receiving
" their visits, and holding long conferences
" with them in his house; ordering his
" servants to bring him word directly when
" they came, and recommending also to his
" people an extraordinary secrecy upon the
" subject of these reciprocal conferences.

" 4thly,

"4thly, It is proved, that the conse-
"quences of this reconciliation with the
"jesuits, were, first, that they also decla-
"red themselves enemies to the king and
"his government; secondly, that they una-
"nimously agreed, at the conferences held
"at St. Anthony's and St. Rock's, and in
"Joseph Mascarenias's house, that the only
"means of changing the government was to
"contrive the death of the king, treating
"this project as the common cause, the je-
"suits assuring the prisoner, that there was
"no fear of his suffering for this attempt, as,
"when the king was once dead, all would
"be soon hushed up, and giving it as their
"opinion, that the murder of the king would
"not be even a *venial* sin, with other maxims
"of the same nature, which would be too
"offensive to pious ears, were they to be
"mentioned. All this shocking doctrine
"being maintained in repeated meetings of
"this prisoner, the jesuits and other ac-
"complices of the conspiracy.

"5thly,

" 5thly, It is proved, that the said pri-
" soner and the jesuits got into their plot
" Leonora de Tavora, late marchioness of
" the same title; and this, notwithstanding
" her old and settled aversion from Joseph
" Mascarenias, arising from difference of hu-
" mours, opposition of interest, and a kind
" of rivalship in pride and ambition: But,
" although their reciprocal aversion was
" increased by his endeavouring to deprive
" her husband, Francisco de Assis de Tavora,
" of the estate of Magaride, and of the
" free lands of his family during his absence
" in the Indies; yet, notwitstanding all
" this, the malice of the jesuits, and the
" malignity of this criminal were of
" force sufficient to induce the said Leo-
" nora de Tavora to enter into this infamous
" conspiracy.

" 6thly, It is proved that the late mar-
" chioness being entered into the plot, both
" she and the jesuits labored to persuade all
" their

" their friends that Gabriel Malagrida the
" jesuit was a saint. In consequence of
" which the late marchioness performed her
" spiritual exercises under his direction, and
" made a show of following all his councils,
" causing thereby the following pernicious
" evils : 1st, that her house became a daily
" assembly of murmurers against the king;
" 2dly, that the common conversation in
" her house was of treasons and plots against
" the king; many schemes being contrived
" for executing the desired assassination;
" 3dly, that the marchioness embraced a
" conformity of detestable sentiments with
" Joseph Mascarenias; making agreements
" at the said late duke's house for killing
" the king; 4thly, that the marchioness en-
" tered into a confederacy, not only with
" her constant director Malagrida, but also
" with the jesuits John de Matos, John
" Alexander, and others; 5thly, that she
" made herself one of the three chiefs of
" this conspiracy, and got into it by her
                                    " authority

" authority and artifice, and the methods
" before mentioned, all those persons she
" could impose upon; 6thly, that she asso-
" ciated herself to the perpetrators of the
" assassination of the third of September,
" by giving sixteen moidores, as part of
" their reward, to those infamous and de-
" testable monsters, who, in that fatal
" night, did the sacrilegious deed, for which
" we all now weep.

" 7thly, It is proved, that as she had
" gained a despotic ascendant over her hus-
" band, sons, daughters, and son in law;
" she got into the plot, and engaged in the
" assassination her husband, sons, son in law,
" brothers in law, and friends, using as an
" instrument so to do, not only the opinion
" she had attempted to spread of Malagrida's
" sanctity, but also certain letters Malagri-
" da used to write to her, desiring her to
" induce all her relations to come to Setuval
" to

PORTUGAL, SPAIN, &c. 79

" to make their spiritual exercises under his
" direction.

" 8thly, The first that was drawn into
" this horrid plot was Francisco de Assis de
" Tavora, late marquis of the same name,
" deluded by these chiefs of the conspiracy,
" his wife, the late duke of Aveiro, and
" the jesuits. He mixed in all their confer-
" ences in the before mentioned places, and
" gave twelve moidores to the late duke, as
" his quota of the reward to the assassins.
" In particular, it is proved that he was in
" one of the parties posted in the fields to
" kill the king; that after the assassination
" he was seeen in the field behind the late
" duke's garden, talking with the other ac-
" complices of the assassination, and was
" present next morning at the meeting in the
" said garden, where some found fault with
" the assassins for not doing their work ef-
" fectually, and the late marquis and others
" boasted, that the king should not have es-
" caped

" caped them, had he paſſed by the
" place where they were poſted.

" 9thly, The ſecond drawn into this con-
" ſpiracy, by the ſame perſons and the ſame
" means, was the late marquis Louis Ber-
" nardo de Tavora. Againſt him it is proved,
" that he was preſent at all the aforeſaid
" conferences, and offered arms and horſes to
" execute the aſſaſſination, two days before
" which he ſent two horſes ſecretly, with all
" their furniture, to the late duke's ſtables.
" Moreover, upon the fatal day, September
" the third in the evening, he was ſhut up
" in private conference with his father and
" brother Joſeph Maria de Tavora, contrary
" to his cuſtom, after which he was in one
" of the parties poſted to kill the king; and
" next morning at the before mentioned
" meeting of the conſpirators at the late
" duke's houſe.

10thly, The

" 10thly, The third drawn into the plot
" by the fame means and fame perfons, was
" the late count of Atouguia, fon in law to
" the late marquis and marchionefs of Tavo-
" ra. It is proved, that he, with his wife,
" were prefent every night at the before
" mentioned conferences, and that he gave
" eight moidores to the affaffins, as his quota
" of their reward; that he was in one of the
" parties pofted to kill the king, and that
" he and his wife were prefent the next
" morning at the late duke of Aveiro's.

" 11thly, The fourth drawn into the plot,
" by the fame means and fame perfons, was
" Jofeph Maria de Tavora, aid de camp to
" his father, the late marquis of Tavora. It
" is proved againft this unhappy youth, that
" he was in one of the parties pofted to kill
" the king; and that after the horrid at-
" tempt was made he affifted at the council
" of the accomplices holden upon the fpot,
" on the north fide of the late duke of Avei-
" ro's

" ro's garden, near the pallifades which you
" muft pafs to enter his houfe. He was
" moreover at the meeting next morning,
" and upon their talking of the miraculous
" manner in which the king's life was pre-
" ferved; he pronounced the following bar-
" barous and facrilegious words: " For my
" part, he fhould not have efcaped me."

" 12thly, The fifth perfon concerned
" was Bras Jofeph Romeiro, by whofe con-
" feflion it appears, that he had lived with
" the late marquis of Tavora from the year
" 1749, had accompanied him when he
" went viceroy to the Indies, and after his
" return had ferved the young marquis, his
" eldeft fon, being a corporal in his compa-
" ny, clerk of his kitchen, and a great fa-
" vourite. It appears moreover, by his con-
" feflion, that the late young marquis had
" told him what had paffed in their meet-
" ing, the evening before the affaflination;
" that both the late marquiffes, father and
" fon,

" son, ordered him to lead the horses they
" had prepared, to the place where their
" most execrable crime was to be perpetrated.
" That he was to adjust the different parties,
" and that he placed himself in one of them
" together with the late marquis of Tavora,
" the father; and that he was in the extem-
" porary council holden to the north side of
" the late duke's garden.

" 13thly, The sixth and seventh drawn
" into this conspiracy, by Joseph Mascare-
" nias (heretofore duke of Aveiro) were An-
" tonio Alvarez Ferreira, who was formerly
" valet de chambre to the said Joseph Mas-
" carenias, and Joseph Policarpio de Azeve-
" do, brother in law to Antonio Alvarez
" Ferreira. It is fully proved, that Joseph
" Mascarenias sent his present valet de
" chambre, Emanuel Alvarez Ferreira, to
" call Antonio Alvarez Ferreira his bro-
" ther; to which latter he opened the affair
" in a hut behind his house at Bellem, with
" great charges of secrecy, ordering him to
" way-

" way-lay the king's chaise, and fire at it
" jointly with him. But Joseph Mascare-
" nias and Antonio Alvarez Ferreira after-
" wards agreed, that he, the said Antonio,
" should speak to his brother in law Joseph
" Policarpio to be their accomplice. In ef-
" fect he spoke to this said Joseph Policarpio,
" and both of them settled and concerted af-
" fairs with Joseph Mascarenias, with whom
" they frequently went both on foot and
" horseback, in order that he might shew them
" and make them know the king's chaise. He
" also ordered them to buy two unknown
" horses, which Antonio Alvarez Ferreira
" bought, one of Lewis de Horta, who lives in
" the Patio do Socorro, for four moidores; the
" other of a gipsey, called Emanuel Soares,
" who lives in Meravilla, for four moidores
" and a half. The said Joseph Mascarenias
" also ordered them to buy unknown arms,
" but Antonio Alvarez Ferreira did not buy
" them, for he and his brother in law made
" use of a blunderbuss of his own, and ano-
" ther

" ther that he borrowed, and two piftols
" which he borrowed, under pretence of
" trying them, of a foreigner, that lives in
" the houfe of the count of Unhaon, and
" foon after the attempt reftored them.
" Thefe were the arms with which Antonio
" Alvarez Ferreira and Jofeph Policarpio
" fired at the king's chaife. The reward
" which thefe two affaffins received for their
" bloody work, from Jofeph Mafcarenias,
" was forty moidores, fixteen at one time,
" four at another, and twenty at another.
" Immediately after having fired at the
" king's chaife, they ran over the fields till
" they got to the paved road without the
" Quinta de Meyo, which road they foon
" left, to turn up the lane of the Guarda-
" mor da Saude, and fo retired to Lifbon.
" Two days after Antonio Alvarez Ferreira
" went to the late duke's houfe, who had
" fent for him, and who told him peevifhly,
" that his fire was good for nothing, add-
" ing, moreover, with his finger laid upon
" his

" his mouth, and much at his ease, " that
" the devil himself could not know what
" they had done, if he did not discover it;"
" and he told him not to sell the horses im-
" mediately, to avoid suspicion. So that
" Antonio Alvarez Ferreira, and Joseph Po-
" licarpio, his brother in law, were, un-
" doubtedly, those horrid monsters that dis-
" charged the pieces, which wounded the
" sacred person of his majesty.

" 14thly, It is proved, that the eighth
" person drawn into this conspiracy by Jo-
" seph Mascarenias, was Emanuel Alvarez
" Ferreira, who often went to tell his bro-
" ther Antonio Alvarez Ferreira, the assas-
" sin, to come to the said Joseph Mascare-
" nias. This person got the cloak and wig
" in which Joseph Mascarenias was disguis-
" ed the night of the assassination. More-
" over he concealed the certain knowledge
" he had from his brother of the conspi-
" racy three or four days after the fact
" was

" was committed, till he was apprehended.
" It was he too that in the Quinta* de Azei-
" taon drew his fword againſt the magiſtrate
" Lewis Antonio de Leiro, as he was
" with no lefs honor than refolution at-
" tempting to ſtop the flight of Joſeph Maſ-
" carenias.

" 15th, It is proved, that the ninth af-
" fociate, led into this plot by the before
" mentioned chiefs, was John Miguel, foot-
" man and confident of Joſeph Mafcarenias.
" It was known, that one of the name of
" John was with Joſeph Mafcarenias at the
" time of the affaffination ; and it appears,
" by his his maſter's own declaration, that
" it was John Miguel, who was with him
" under the arch when he the faid Joſeph
" Mafcarenias took aim againſt the king's
" poſtilion, and drew the trigger, but his
" piece miſſed fire.

* Quinta is a villa, or country houfe.

" 16thly,

"16thly, It is proved, that the three fore-
"mentioned chiefs of this conspiracy execut-
"ed the same by the assistance of all these
"confederates in the following manner."

LETTER XIV.

LISBON, FEB. 16, 1759.

" 17thly, IT is proved, that after the
" two chiefs of this horrid conspiracy,
" Joseph Mascarenias and Leonora de Ta-
" vora, had raised the never enough to be
" detested collection, to the making up of
" which the above mentioned accomplices
" contributed, so that in all they raised the
" trifling sum of 192 millrees" (30 pieces of
36 shillings, or 40 moidores), " which was
" given as their reward to the two barbarous
" assassins, Antonio Alvarez Ferreira and Jo-
" seph Policarpio; and after that Louis Ber-
" nardo de Tavora had sent his two horses
" with their furniture to the stables of Jo-
" seph Mascarenias the same night of the
" assassination, to which same stables Fran-
" cis

"cis de Aſſis de Tavora likewiſe ſent three
"other horſes, which were left there by
"his poſtilion and Bras Joſeph Romeiro
"the corporal; and after that the before
"mentioned Joſeph Maſcarenias, the ſame
"night of the aſſaſſination, had likewiſe
"prepared, and ſent into the fields lying
"behind the wood-built houſe of Antonio
"Joſeph de Matos his ſecretary, the other
"horſes neceſſary, which were taken from
"his own ſtables, and called Serra and
"Guardamor, with two other unmarked
"horſes" (the horſes of blood in theſe countries are always marked upon one haunch)
"called Palhavan and Coimbra, which with
"the horſes bought by the two aſſaſſins,
"Antonio Alvarez Ferreira and Joſeph Po-
"licarpio, made up the number of eleven;
"after all theſe things the eleven copartners
"of this horrid impiety went and mount-
"ed them, placing themſelves in differ-
"ent ambuſcades along that little ſpace of
"ground which lies between the north end
"of

" of the Quinta de Meyo, and the south
" end of the Quinta de Cim, by which the
" king usually returns home when he has
" been out in private.

" 18thly, It is proved, that just as the
" king had turned the corner of the north
" wall of the Quinta de Meyo, as soon as
" ever he was come from under the arch
" which stood in that place," (it is now pulled down as having given shelter to so atrocious a deed) " the said chief of the conspi-
" racy Joseph Mascarenias, who was in com-
" pany with his servant and confident John
" Miguel, and another of the criminals, ad-
" vanced a little forwards, and shot off his pis-
" tol or blunderbuss, taking aim at Custodio
" da Costa the postilion, who was driving his
" majesty, but his piece missed fire. The
" postilion hearing the noise of the trigger's
" going down, and seeing the sparks fly from
" the flint, without saying any thing to the
" king, galloped on with his mules as fast
" as

" as ever he could in order to avoid a second
" fire, as he saw the former attempt was
" aimed at his life. Now Joseph Mascare-
" nias's piece missing fire was the first mira-
" cle which divine Omnipotence operated in
" favor of these realms; for had the posti-
" lion been killed, the life of his most
" sacred majesty would have been in the
" power of those horrid monsters then in
" arms, and in ambuscades so closely set
" against his august person and most pre-
" cious life.

" 19thly, It is proved, that upon account
" of the postilion's going so very fast, the
" two barbarous assassins, Antonio Alvarez
" Ferreira and Joseph Policarpio, who were
" standing a little way below Joseph Mas-
" carenias, at the end of the new wall,
" could not take so good aim as they wished
" at the chaise, and were obliged to follow
" it on full gallop, in order to fire off their
" pieces

"pieces as well as they could againſt the
"back of it. It was by theſe two never
"enough to be deteſted parricides that the
"auguſt perſon of his majeſty was wounded
"quite from his ſhoulder down his arm to
"the elbow, both on the inſide and out,
"beſides a great deal of fleſh being carried
"away; nay, his breaſt was even torn, and
"a number of ſhot were afterwards ex-
"tracted from it. For, to ſhew the cruelty
"of theſe aſſaſſins, inſtead of charging
"their pieces with balls, they filled them
"with very large ſhot, to render their ſa-
"vage and never ſufficiently to be abhorred
"deſign more certain. This was the ſecond
"miracle which divine Omnipotence operated
"in that fatal night, to the common benefit
"and advantage of theſe kingdoms. For
"in the common courſe of things it is not to
"be conceived how two ſuch charges ſhould
"paſs through a ſmall chaiſe without de-
"ſtroying the perſons who were in it.

"20th,

" 20th, The king, to avoid the three de-
" lays, of going to the palace, fending for
" the furgeon, and then the delay of his
" coming, ordered the poftilion to turn about
" and drive directly to his furgeon general's
" houfe, by which means his majefty, thro'
" an extraordinary providence, efcaped the
" other parties that were laid in wait for
" him.

" 21ft, It is proved, that Jofeph Mafcarenias
" and the reft that were lying in wait for the
" king, retired immediately by private paths
" to the road that paffes by the north end
" of his garden, boafting among themfelves
" of what they had done; and the late
" duke beating his blunderbufs againft a
" ftone, and faying, " the devil take you,
" when I want you moft, you do me no
" fervice!" And when Francis de Affis, the
" late marquis of Tavora, expreffed a doubt
" whether the king was killed or no, the
" late duke replied, " it does not fignify, if
" he

" he is not dead, die he shall." Another
" answered, our point is to find him from
" home, &c. Joseph Maria de Tavora also
" very much at his own ease inquired for
" John Miguel, and why he was not come
" up, which he did a very little time after.
" The next day the infatuated council of
" the accomplices met at the late duke of
" Aveiro's house, in which some boasted of
" what they had done; others accused the
" assassins of bungling; others said that the
" king should not have escaped them, had
" he gone on the usual road, and not turned
" back down the paved road of the Ajuda,
" towards the Junquicra.

" 22d, Although all the foregoing cir-
" cumstances had not been fully proved, as
" many of them rarely are in cases of the
" like nature, tho' in this affair by a fresh
" and evident miracle the horrid impieties
" of each criminal are fully verified; yet,
" even without such ample proofs, certain
" pre-

" presumptions of the laws would have
' been sufficient for the condemnation of
" the criminals; of which presumptions
" there are many to be made against the
" chiefs of this conspiracy, and especially
" against the jesuits, and the heretofore
" duke of Aveiro.

" 23d, It is presumed, in confirmation of
" what we have laid down in the foregoing
" articles, that he who has once been bad,
" will always be bad in the same kind of
" wickedness as that he before committed.
" Now not only once, but many have been
" the iniquities that these two chiefs of the
" conspiracy, the jesuits and Joseph Masca-
" renias, have plotted against the government
" of our sovereign lord the king, by a series
" of facts from the very beginning of his
" reign.

" 24th, Moreover with regard to the je-
" suits, as they saw, by reason of the great
" supe-

"superiority of sense and discernment in
"our present sovereign, that it was impossi-
"ble for them to preserve in this court the
"despotism to which they pretended, and
"knowing also that without this absolute
"power there were no means of covering
"their usurpations in Portuguese Asia, Afri-
"ca, and America, much less of palliating
"the war that they had kindled by a formal
"rebellion in the northern and southern
"parts of the Brazils; seeing this, they
"contrived against the reputation of his ma-
"jesty and the public repose of these king-
"doms the most calumnious and detestable
"suggestions and intrigues ever known, to
"alienate, by these means, from their
"affection to his majesty as well natives as
"foreigners, and have several times at-
"tempted divers execrable projects in order
"to excite sedition, and bring the scourge
"of war upon these realms. From all
"which it is concluded that the jesuits hav-
"ing committed these impieties against the

"king

" king and his kingdoms, fall exactly under
" the beforementioned rule and presumption
" of law, that he who has been once bad
" will always remain so, in the same kind
" of wickedness; and even if the principal
" proofs were wanting, they would always
" be presumed to have contrived the assassi-
" nation, till they can shew others against
" whom there are equal presumptions.

" 25th, The law moreover presumes, that
" no person would commit a crime, with-
" out having a great interest in the com-
" mission of it. It is moreover presumed,
" that he who has the greatest interest in a
" crime is the author of it, till he can shew
" who was the author, or justify himself.
" Now the jesuits having, as we have be-
" fore said, the greatest interest in this con-
" spiracy, in order to change the present
" government, by depriving the king of his
" life, this bare presumption of law would
" be sufficient to repute them guilty of this

" execrable

"execrable treason, without they can justify
"themselves.

"26th, But all the proofs and presump-
"tions here laid down are most exceedingly
"strengthened, when it is considered, that
"while the king was disconcerting the be-
"fore mentioned plots of the jesuits, and
"dismissing the confessors he had of that
"order, and forbidding them to enter the
"palace, during all these proceedings, in-
"stead of humbling themselves upon ac-
"count of so many restrictions, on the
"contrary their arrogance visibly increased,
"boasting publicly, that their being forbid-
"den the court signified little while noble-
"men sought them in their cloysters, and
"that the avenging hand of Heaven hung
"heavy over the former, suggesting that the
"life of his majesty would be short, and
"spreading about rumours by means of all
"their followers, that he would not live to
"the end of the month of August, writing

"the

"the same in frequent letters to different
"parts of the globe, nay, even adding that
"September was at farthest to be the fatal
"month in which the precious life of his
"majesty was to end. Gabriel Malagrida
"in particular wrote similar prognostications
"in the tone of prophecies to several people
"of this court. However they entirely al-
"tered their manner of speaking and writ-
"ing, upon the nobles being arrested, which
"was in the morning of the thirteenth of
"December last. The following post day
"for Italy, the nineteenth of the same
"month, the provincial father John Hen-
"riques wrote to Rome, as well as others
"of the said order, who instead of haughty
"terms, and prophecies of death and re-
"venge, which were so frequent in their
"mouths before, in this post made use
"of much more submissive expressions, tel-
"ling their friends that the marquisses of
"Tavora, the duke of Aveiro, the marquis
"of Alorna, the count of Atouguia, and
"others,

" others, had been taken up on account of
" the king's being shot at on the third of
" September, adding, that soldiers were
" placed at all their convents, and begging
" their brethren in Rome to recommend
" them to Heaven, of whose assistance they
" stood in need, as not being able to resist
" the storm which they feared was going to
" break upon their heads. That all their
" brotherhood was very much afflicted, and
" recurred for comfort to the spiritual exer-
" cises of father Malagrida. That the
" world esteemed them as accomplices of
" the fatal attack of the third of September,
" and had already condemned them in their
" own imaginations either to be imprisoned,
" or exterminated and totally expelled the
" court and kingdom. That they were in
" the greatest streights, and reduced to the
" greatest calamities, full of fears and an-
" xieties, without any comfort or hope of
" being relieved from them, &c. Now this
" contradictory behaviour of the jesuits be-
" fore

"fore and after the shooting of the king
"is a *clear demonstration* that before the said
"attack they had confidence in their con-
"spiracy, and therefore spoke and wrote
"with so much pride and spiritual arrogance,
"issuing out their horrible and sacrilegious
"prophecies. But after the seizure of the
"nobles on the thirteenth of December,
"and the guards being set at their convents,
"seeing themselves discovered, and those
"they had stirred up to be their accom-
"plices lost, and upon the verge of being
"punished, they fell, with all their chime-
"rical ideas of greatness, into that lowness
"of spirits which is the constant attendant
"upon the being guilty of a crime without
"knowing how to cover it.

27th, (The foregoing presumptions of law are produced against the duke of Aveiro, after which my author goes on thus:) "But
"he fell from that height of pride and arro-
"gance as soon as he found the conspiracy
"had

"had failed; and not having resolution
"enough to appear at court, he retired to
"the Quinta de Arataon, where he was
"taken, after having first attempted to save
"himself by flight, and afterwards by a
"vain resistance.

"28th, The same presumptions hold
"good, likewise, with regard to Donna
"Leonora de Tavora, heretofore marchioness
"of that title, and the third principal in
"this horrid conspiracy. Her proud spirit
"and insatiable ambition were notorious.
"She was of a more daring and intrepid
"disposition than was ever seen in persons
"of her sex, and therefore capable of incit-
"ing and undertaking the most desperate
"attempts. Hurried away by her blind,
"tho' ardent passions, she and her husband
"supplicated the king to give them some
"dukedom, tho' the insignificant services
"they had done to his majesty had been
"amply

" amply recompensed by sending the late
" marquis viceroy to India; for an example
" is not to be found in all the annals of this
" kingdom, of the title of duke being ever
" given for services of much greater conse-
" quence, as were those of many and very
" great heroes, who have adorned the history of
" Portugal by their illustrious deeds. These
" two criminals were, moreover, always
" persecuting the secretary of state in a
" public manner, without regard or shame,
" to grant the aforesaid title, to which they
" had so absolutely insignificant pretensions;
" yet they continued to demand it as a debt
" that was by justice due to them, which
" obliged the secretary to check their im-
" portunate entreaties and reasonings, by
" telling them in a civil and honorable
" manner, that there was no precedent of
" any such title being conferred for such
" kind of services. It was this necessary
" truth that first hurried the marchioness
" into

" into her alliance with the duke of Aveiro,
" hoping by his means, after the death of
" the king, to be able to enjoy that title she
" so much desired, and which she so much
" envied him. And it is manifest to every
" person, that all this pride, haughtiness and
" ambition with which she behaved, before
" the horrid action of the third of September, fell into that langour and confusion
" which attends a guilty conscience when
" the crime is discovered.

" 29th, All the above mentioned proofs
" having been thoroughly examined, his
" majesty in conjunction with his council,
" to whom he has for that end given a
" larger jurisdiction and authority, in order
" that they may be able to inflict punish-
" ments in some measure adequate to the
" execrable and scandalous crimes of the
" before mentioned infamous and sacrile-
" gious criminals, decree———,

Then

Then follows the sentence, which I will give you in my next paper, and if I can shorten it a little I will, tho' I am desirous you should see the whole form and ceremony of our proceedings in this country. I will make no remarks upon the presumptions of law alledged towards the latter end of this paper, as you will be better able to do it than myself.

LETTER XV.

LISBON, FEB. 20, 1759.

"WE sentence the criminal Joseph Mas-
"carenias, late duke of Aveiro, who has
"been already outlawed, and deprived of all
"the honors of a Portuguese and vassal to
"his majesty, degraded from the order of
"St. Jago, and delivered over to the court
"and the arm of secular justice here admi-
"nistered, as one of the three chiefs or
"principal authors of this infamous con-
"spiracy, as well as of the horrid assault
"which was the effect of it; we, therefore,
"sentence him to be conducted publicly
"with a halter about his neck to the square
"of the key or mole of Bellem, and there,
"upon a high scaffold for that purpose to be
"erected, in order that his punishment may
"be in view of the whole people, so much
"offended

" offended by the scandal of his most inju-
" rious crimes, shall he be racked alive, by
" breaking the bones of his legs and arms
" both great and small, to the number of
" eight; after which he shall be exposed
" upon a wheel for the satisfaction of the
" present and future subjects of these king-
" doms, which being done the aforesaid cri-
" minal shall be burnt alive, together with
" the scaffold upon which he was executed,
" till the whole shall by fire be reduced to
" dust and ashes, which shall be thrown into
" the sea, in order that of him and his
" memory no traces may be left. More-
" over all his estates real and personal are
" confiscated, his coat of arms is to be
" beaten down or erased wherever it is
" found, his name to be cancelled where-
" ever it is written, all his houses and other
" edifices to be demolished and razed to the
" ground, so as not to have the least mark
" of them left, but the places are to be re-
" duced

" duced into fields, and falt fcattered upon
" the fpot where they ftood.

" We fentence the criminal Francis de
" Affis de Tavora, late marquis of the fame
" title, chief alfo of the confpiracy, into
" which he was drawn by the perfuafions
" of his wife, to the like punifhment with
" Jofeph Mafcarenias, having been pre-
" vioufly in the fame manner outlawed and
" deprived of the honors of a Portuguefe.
" We too, having reflected, with the feri-
" oufnefs and circumfpection neceffary in
" affairs of this nature, that the faid crimi-
" nal and his wife were not only perfonal
" actors in this horrible confpiracy, treafon
" and parricide, but by their artifices made
" the enormous crime common to the reft
" of their family, arriving therein at their
" aim, and perverting the greateft part of
" their faid family to their wicked in-
" tentions; and boafting with idle and
" overbearing vanity, that their union alone
" would

" would be sufficient to effect their diabolical
" machinations, decree, that no person, of
" whatever state or condition, shall after
" the publication of this sentence dare to use
" the sirname of Tavora, under pain of all
" his goods being confiscated, and himself
" outlawed and banished from the king-
" doms and dominions of Portugal, thereby
" losing all the privileges that now belong
" to him as a native thereof.

" As for the two savage monsters Antonio
" Alvarez Ferreira and Joseph Policarpio de
" Azevedo, who discharged those pieces from
" which the supreme majesty of the king
" received his wounds, we sentence them
" to be conducted with halters about their
" necks to the aforesaid square of Bellem,
" where, after being chained to two high
" poles erected for that purpose, they are to
" be surrounded with fire, which is to con-
" sume them alive, till their bodies shall be
" reduced to dust and ashes, to be thrown
" into

"into the sea as before expressed. More-
"over their goods are confiscated, and the
"houses in which they dwelt are to be de-
"molished and destroyed, supposing, how-
"ever, they are their own property, in
"which case salt is likewise to be scattered
"upon the place where they stood. And
"as the criminal Joseph Policarpio is not
"to be found, we here proscribe him and
"declare him outlawed, and order all the
"magistrates in the kingdom, in their respec-
"tive towns to summon the inhabitants
"together, in order to find him out and ap-
"prehend him, or in case of their not being
"able to take him alive, to kill him, sup-
"posing, however, that the person who kills
"him be not his enemy. And the person
"or persons who shall bring the said Jo-
"seph Policarpio alive to Pedro Gonsalvez
"Cordeiro Pereira, justiciary of high trea-
"son within this realm, shall receive at
"sight the reward of ten thousand new
"crowns;" (a new crown is something
above

above half a crown English) " supposing
" him to be taken in the dominions of this
" kingdom; or of twenty thousand crowns if
" taken in any foreign country, besides be-
" ing repaid the expences they may have
" incurred in bringing him to the aforesaid
" senator Pedro Gonsalvez Cordeiro Pereira.

" We sentence moreover the following
" criminals, Louis Bernardo de Tavora, Don
" Jeronymo de Ataide, late count of Atou-
" guia, Joseph Maria de Tavora, Bras Jo-
" seph Romeiro, John Miguel, and Ema-
" nuel Alvarez Ferreira, to be conducted
" with halters about their necks to the scaf-
" fold to be erected for these executions,
" where they shall be strangled first, after
" which the great and small bones of their
" arms and legs shall be broken, and laid
" upon wheels, and their bodies reduced by
" fire into ashes, which shall be thrown in-
" to the sea as above mentioned. More-
" over all their estates real and personal, and
" other

" other goods are confiscated, and perpetual
" infamy is intailed upon their children and
" posterity. The houses where they dwel-
" led, supposing them to be their own pro-
" perty, are to be demolished and rased to
" the ground, and salt scattered upon the
" spot where they stood. Moreover the
" coats of arms that any of these criminals
" have borne to this time, are to be beaten
" down to the ground and erased.

" Lastly, we sentence the criminal Leo-
" nora de Tavora, wife of the criminal
" Francis de Assis de Tavora, excusing her
" upon just considerations from the severe
" punishments her crimes deserve, to be
" conducted with a halter about her
" neck to the before mentioned scaffold,
" where her head shall be severed from her
" body, both which shall afterwards be re-
" duced by fire to ashes, to be thrown like-
" wise into the sea. Moreover all her estates
" real and personal are confiscated, and all

" the other punishments are to take place
" in her denounced against the criminal Jo-
" seph Mascarenias, and Francis de Assis de
" Tavora, in order to blot out entirely the
" memory of there having been such persons
" upon the face of the earth.

" At the palace of our lady of help, in the
" meeting of the 12th of January 1759,
" signed with the seals of the three secreta-
" ries of state who presided at it, with the
" names of the following judges under-
" written:

Cordeiro
Pacheco,
Bacalhaon,
Lima,   } were present."
Souto,
Oliveira,
Machado,

Then comes the royal seal, which concludes the whole.

Most of the goods and furniture of the unfortunate noblemen who were executed have been selling by auction, and the English say in a bad manner, nay that even every thing most trifling, as dirty caps and such things, were included in the sale. Some other nobles are to be banished, and the rest that are in prison to be released. The king has granted for life to his secretary of state Sebastian Joseph de Carvalho forty body guards, who ride after his chaise with their swords drawn, &c. An officer with a drummer attending him and beating at their head render him a very pompous figure. The reason assigned for this is lest any of the family of the poor nobles should chuse to revenge their death upon him, whom every person esteems the author of it. However, I fancy a little ambition is at the bottom, as to defend himself from a stilletto four guards would do as well as four hundred. The ladies that were wives or other relations to the nobles are still in monasteries, from whence I should think they would not chuse to come out even if they could. The young marchioness of Tavora is likewise in a convent, she who is supposed to be the real spring of all this mystery; and you see in what the court has published, tho' they tell you exactly where the king was going, yet they say nothing of whence he came at that time of night without any guards or even a servant to attend him, and only an unknown person in the chaise. Indeed, without something of that sort, the whole story would be incoherent, for that the Tavora family should be so stirred up against the king, because his minister would not make them dukes, seems a thing difficult to be believed. What appears to me most particular is, that tho' the king was known to frequent the young marchioness for above three years before, yet this flame of Portuguese revenge should break out so late. This can only be attributed to the jesuits, who with all their art blew up this terrible combustion,

buſtion, in revenge for what had juſtly been done to them, for their incroachments in South America. What is become of the heads of them nobody knows. We have expected every day to ſee a new execution, and Malagrida with ſome of the other principals of that order at the head of it. But nothing has yet appeared. We know that guards are ſet at all their convents, that when any of them is to ſay maſs, two ſoldiers ſtand on each ſide of the altar. We know that a great many are in priſon, but this is all we know for certain, the reſt is only conjecture. If I can get any thing tolerably authentic about them for my next paper I will ſend it you. One of the principal of them is ſaid to have died a natural death in priſon a few days ago, but whether his end was ſo or no I cannot tell, however I have heard that he was in a lingering way before. Among the common people there is a rumour, that a good many of them have been put to death ſecretly.

LISBON, FEB. 24, 1759.

I AM glad that my letters concerning our conspiracy meet so much with your approbation. You will by this time have received some more, and I have, perhaps, one or two still remaining, but I must wait a little, to get more authentic intelligence. What I have written was from the truest informations I could possibly obtain. The court attempts to throw a veil over all its actions, and you only find against whom its anger is turned, as the bolts fall.

These mysterious proceedings render the Portuguese very shy of speaking about public affairs; and, indeed, the English factory has but little connection with them. This will hinder

hinder me from being able to know so much of their manners as I could wish; for, I confess, I should be pleased to know the descendants of those heroes, whose arms made the Moors tremblingly relinquish their possessions in Africa; and whose fleets urging on through unknown seas to farthest India erected an empire which might still have flourished, if their falling under the yoke of Philip the second had not sunk that national spirit, which seems never to have been thoroughly roused again. When, indeed, they broke their chains and set the house of Braganza upon the throne in the reign of Philip the fourth of Spain, they maintained a long war against the irritated Spaniard, but after treaties had established their independence, they sunk again into inactivity. This seems still to hang upon them, and will probably do so, till some new exertion calls them forth to action, which seems difficult, however, to happen in our times, as their trade will always find them protectors who will fight for them. The race of those who fought for themselves, seems in part to have perished with the Alonsos and Sebastians.

The same rumour prevails here as with you in London, of the death of the king of Spain; and that they conceal it in order to give the king of Naples more time to regulate his affairs. The other day there was a little dispute between captain Legge and one of the Disimbargadors. Captain Legge commands the Trident, a ship belonging to Admiral Holmes's division of Saunders's squadron, and which, by the bad weather, was driven into this port dismasted. He had three Portuguese subjects on board. One of them one night wanted to desert, and accordingly, had got down into the Tagus to swim on shore, but being observed, was retaken, and by captain Legge's orders put into irons for four and twenty hours. In the mean time his two countrymen contrived to send a note to Lisbon of there being three Portuguese subjects on board, who they said had been very ill treated, and that the captain would not dismiss them, tho' they had begged him repeated times to do it. The Disimbargador or magistrate of justice, to whom this complaint was made, ordered his officers to arrest captain Legge as soon as he came on shore, styling him in his warrant captain of a privateer, whether thro' ignorance or cunning, not to have been said to have put under arrest an officer in his Britannic majesty's service, I know not. However, certain it was, that the order was given; but the officer that was commissioned to put it in execution, acquainted a friend of captain Legge's of the whole affair, who informed him of it. He immediately wrote a letter to our consul, complaining of the insult that had been offered to the British flag. The affair, however, has been set to rights, and the Disimbargador reprimanded. As for the

the three Portuguese, I do not know whether they have been yet delivered or not, but I believe they will, as I think Carvalho has issued those orders.

LETTER XVII.

LISBON, FEB. 25, 1759.

I promised you some further account of the affair of the conspiracy in these countries, but as a deep cloud seems still to overwhelm what concerns the jesuits, which is all that remains, I will wait another week in hopes of its dissipating. With regard to the nobles, I think there is nothing more to add. Some indeed, they say, have been relegated to St. Thomé, or other distant parts of the Portuguese dominions, and the remainder are still in prison.

To turn your eyes, therefore, from this melancholy subject, and give you the former glories, as I have sent you the present misfortunes of Portugal, I will speak of what

it

it was heretofore. This I will do in confequence of your defiring me to give you some
hiftorical account of the countries I paffed
thro'. Tho' I confider your defire as calculated more for my inftruction than for your
own information, I fhall obey your commands.

Portugal is nearly the antient Lufitania of
the Romans, and after the fall of this powerful nation funk, like the reft of its depen-
dencies, under the hands of thofe barbarous
emigrants, who overthrew what the idle fancy
of the Latin authors had deemed eternal.
To the Vifigoths, or weftern Goths, who
occupied Spain, fucceeded the Saracens, who
had embraced a religion which was to be pro-
pagated by conqueft, and who coming directly
from Barbary, were at length confounded
with the inhabitants of that country and called Moors. Long did a few oppreffed be-
lievers groan under this yoke, till at length
count Alonfo Enriquez, by his victories over

the

the disciples of Mahomet, formed a little territory, which he ruled with the title of king given him by pope Eugenius III. His successors increased the territories, and established the kingdom of Portugal, whose history, however, yielded nothing very remarkable for a long time, except wars against the Moors and their neighbours, till at length its maritime situation and the intrepidity of the inhabitants, began to explore what hitherto had lain hid beyond the depths of the ocean. Henry, brother to king John, encouraged these researches, and by his astronomical knowledge and pecuniary largesses had already opened to his countrymen a large part of the coast of Africa. The same spirit seized at length the throne, and John the second sent large expeditions to the astonished negroes, who partly submitted to his arms, and partly embraced his religion. Still farther atchievements were performed by his successor Emanuel, whose triumphant colours passed the cape of Good Hope under

Vasco

Vasco de Gama, and a great part of the East became subject to Portugal. Valor and religion went hand in hand, and soldiers and missionaries shewed equal fanaticism in their different pursuits. In Abyssinia, to their wonder, they found a kingdom already christian, which they converted, with their king David, to the Roman catholic persuasion, but by becoming too assuming, were at last again driven with their tenets out of it. This expulsion was not compleated till the succeeding reigns, and Portugal in other respects continued flourishing till the young Sebastian lost his life and crown in Africa, in the fatal battle against Muley Moluch, whose bravery that day, so fatal to the arms of Portugal, has been sufficiently recorded in history, and particularly in the Spectator. Sebastian likewise shewed himself the hero in that engagement, and was found covered with wounds amongst heaps of the slain, tho' impostors afterwards pretended to be him who had escaped. His crown went to the

the cardinl Henry, who was his great uncle. This prelate was no lefs than fixty-feven years old when he fucceeded to the throne of Portugal, and his fhort reign of not a year and a half was more taken up with difputes about who was to be his fucceffor than any thing elfe. Philip the fecond, then king of Spain, who was one of the candidates, foon defeated the only one of the others who appeared in arms againft him, which was Don Antonio, a baftard fon of the late king's brother. Portugal had no fooner fubmitted to the arms of Spain than all her enthufiafm for glory fell with her independency, and difencouraged, defpifed and oppreffed by her haughty neighbour, fhe feemed to drag on a languifhing exiftence, till the duke of Braganza, under Philip the fourth of Spain, reaffumed the throne of his anceftors by a popular infurrection, and it has ever fince been preferved in that family. But the fpirit of the Portuguefe feems never to have been thoroughly roufed from the lethargy under

which

which it funk during thofe years it was a defpifed province of Spain. They joined with us, however, againft the fucceffion of Philip the fifth, in favor of the houfe of Auftria, but they and their allies were routed at Almanza, fince which time they have performed no active part in Europe. You will be content, I believe, with this fketch, and, indeed, you may, perhaps, not be forry that I have not been more particular.

We fee here all your green houfe plants growing wild in the hedges. Thefe are principally made of aloes, which, indeed, feem more calculated for conftructing a fence than for beauty. They fay, indeed, in England, they are very fine when in flower, but, I believe, only on account of the rarity; as here, where you will foon fee a hundred of them branching out in every lane, no perfon thinks about the matter. The ladies of England have more reafon on their fide with regard to orange trees, as

there

there is something naturally pretty in them, and perhaps more so when they grow in pots than when they are able to attain their full growth, as they acquire a deeper colour, and do not look so lively. As for myrtle it here grows wild in the woods, as neglected a plant as any there.

I shall set out for Seville the beginning of next month, but may stay some days at Beja in my way thither.

LETTER XVIII.

LISBON, MARCH 4, 1759.

THE cloud hanging over the affair of the jesuits is not yet dissipated. I will, therefore, stay another week to see whether it will disperse or no, and in the mean time will send you some account of Camoens the famous Portuguese epic poet, so little known and so much cried up in England, that I have heard him styled the best author in the whole world. Lewis de Camoens was said to be born at Lisbon, but his birth place seems very uncertain. He lived a very unfortunate life, as he was first upon account of some intrigues banished from Lisbon, and went to the Portuguese East Indies, where he afterwards met with a great many disasters, and was by some of the Portuguese

governors

governors banished a second time from their possessions in those countries. Upon this he went to China, and having after some years obtained leave to return to Lisbon, he followed the Portuguese arms into Africa, where he behaved so valiantly, that upon his return he was received very cordially by the famous Sebastian then king of Portugal, to whom he dedicated his poem, the greatest part of which he had composed during the time of his distress, and had preserved when he was cast away upon the coast of Camboya on his returning to Portugal; by swimming on shore with it in his teeth. This was all he saved of what he then possessed in the world. Sebastian gave him a pension for life, upon which he was subsisting very comfortably, when that unfortunate prince lost his life in Africa. Upon the king's perishing Camoens lost likewise his pension, and his successor cardinal Henry dying, all Portugal became a scene of confusion. During this melancholy interval the voice of poor

Camoens remained unheard, and he fell into the moſt extreme poverty. The infirmities attending his advanced age, and the agitation of his ſpirits, ſoon brought him to the grave, and he is even ſaid to have died in an hoſpital. Shortly before he expired he beheld his country fall under the yoke of Spain. Upon this occaſion Camoens in a laſt letter to his friend, a little before his death, uſes theſe words. " I now draw near the
" end of my carreer, and I hope the world
" will have been convinced by my actions of
" my ſincere affection for my country. I reckon
" myſelf happy too, in not only being able
" to die in her boſom, but alſo in not ſur-
" viving her death." He was buried poorly in St. Anne's church, and the following ſimple inſcription was afterwards put upon his grave.

" Here lies Lewis de Camoens, the prince
" of poets in his time, poor and unhappy
                                    " was

"was his life, poor and unhappy was his
" death,
    " In the year 1759."

Having said so much to you about the man, I shall now speak something about his poem, which he entitles the Lusiade, upon account of the Latin name of Portugal, (Lusitania) said to be derived from one Lusus an ancient hero who came here.

The subject of this work is the discovery of the East Indies, tho' he makes very great digressions from it. The Portuguese were the first who, after doubling the Cape of Good Hope, went on towards India. He very nobly represents that famous promontory under the figure of a giant, threatening those hardy mortals who dared to pass his boundaries. The hero of the poem is the first explorer of these unknown seas, Vasco de Gama. The first canto opens in the old style,

style, when Vasco was got about half way to India, which causes an old fashioned quarrel of heathen gods, whether the Portuguese shall accomplish their designs or not. Bacchus is their enemy from jealousy of their going to the Indies, which he is reported formerly to have conquered, lest their victories should obscure his. Venus favors them upon account of their great gallantry. In the mean time Vasco meets with all proper difficulties of winds and weather, and rocks and savages, however, at last Jupiter sends Mercury and Fame to dispose the inhabitants of Melinda on the eastern coast of Africa to be favorable to the adventurers, who land there, and are perfectly well received by the king of that country. As the negro monarch is desirous of being informed of the affairs of Europe, a very long episode is made to explain them, in which Vasco naturally includes those of Portugal, and gives a history of her kings, interspersed with very pretty passages. This long episode concludes

cludes with an account of the voyage of the whole fleet from Portugal, after which the king of Melinda thanks his informer, and they are extremely good friends, till at length Vafco fets forward again in fearch of the rifing fun, for fo our poet generally expreffes himfelf when he fpeaks of the Eaft Indies, Bacchus gets Neptune to raife ftorms, and plays the deuce with him, but at laft they obtain a fight of the long-fought fhores. You may imagine Venus is not idle in affifting them; but notwithftanding her endeavours, when they land upon the coaft of Malabar they cannot agree upon a fettled commerce with the natives, who by the inftigation of Bacchus ufe them very ill, to fuch a degree that they are forced to return without obtaining any other advantage than the being able to give an account of their having difcovered the place defired. In their return Venus throws them upon a delightful ifland, where fhe gets all her friends among the fea nymphs to meet them, and Thetis at their head, who becomes Cicifbea (to ufe an Italian word) to Vafco de Gama. They all are as happy as poffible in the company of their marine divinities, and Thetis carries the officers of the fleet up to the top of a high mountain, where there is a vaft globe reprefenting the univerfe. They here fee all the planetary motions, and all the kingdoms of the earth, and Thetis tells them every thing that is to happen, and in particular with regard to the kingdom of Portugal. After this fupernatural entertainment our heroes quit the ifland and return home, but not without fome difficulties. They are received upon their return with the greateft applaufe.

This is the principal thread of the epic poem, and perhaps I may give you a fhort fample of fome paffages in it. I am too little a judge of the Portuguefe language to give my opinion with regard to the goodnefs of this performance, but at the fame time that I do

not

not deny it has merit, I am far from thinking it one of the beft epic poems in the world, as I have falfely heard it reported to be.

J. E. T.

LETTER XIX.

LISBON, MARCH 8, 1759.

As I have nothing else authentic to write to you for my present paper, I will give you a lame translation of a passage or two of this work of Camoens; chosen out rather from my lighting upon them first, than from their being the best in the poem.

He runs very high in the praise of Alonso the great, king of Portugal, and describes his actions very poetically; I, however, shall only give you here what he says upon his death.

" Alonso, his brows now crowned with
" hoary locks, was enjoying the fruits of
" his glory, when he was obliged to pay

" to

"to the fates that common tribute of nature,
"demanded as well from the king as from
"the shepherd. With inceſſant moan did
"the vaſſals of Portugal lament his death.
"The rocks, woods, and mountains rung
"with their juſt affliction. The Tagus,
"ſwoln with the tears of its nymphs, rolled
"its courſe to the waves of Neptune with
"a melancholy murmur, expreſſive of its
"grief. The echoes with a plaintive voice
"called for a long time upon the generous
"Alonſo; Alonſo, who, tho' dead, yet
"lived in the hearts of his people; and
"left to the univerſe a name indelible by
"the hand of time."

Tho' in a dull proſe tranſlation the original muſt have loſt prodigiouſly, yet, ſtill I hope it will give you ſome little glimmering of what the author would mean to ſay. Some of his deſcriptions of battles are very fine, but deſcriptions of battles are ſuch common—place things in poetry, that I do not

not think it worth while to give you any of them. I rather chuse to give you a little Episode he makes upon the charming Inès, with whom Don Pedro, son of the then reigning Alonso, (quite a different person from him whose death he laments so much,) was in love.

"Alonso, restored once more from Africa
"to his native soil, was preparing to enjoy
"his laurels in tranquillity, when his ease
"and glory were blasted by an unhappy
"event; a fatal and melancholy adventure,
"which rendered the Portuguese spectators
"of beauty unparalleled sinking under the
"weight of unjust rigor. It was thou, O
"far redoubted Love! it was thou alone that
"wast the cause of her death! Thou tyrant
"most cruel, do not the tears of thy slaves
"content thee, but must thou bathe thine
"altars with their blood?

"Thou,

" Thou, O beautiful Inès, upon Mon-
" dego's flowery banks waſt enjoying an
" agreeable ſolitude. Thy lips were teach-
" ing the mountain and foreſt to re-echo
" that beloved name thou boreſt engraven
" on thy heart; the name of thy prince,
" whoſe preſence made thy happineſs, and
" whoſe leaſt abſence coſt thee ſo many
" tears. He too, tho' deprived of thy com-
" pany, felt his whole ſoul occupied with
" the flattering remembrance of thoſe ſweet
" hours he had enjoyed with thee; the
" pledges of his eternal tenderneſs. Tho'
" abſent from thoſe fair eyes, every thing
" brought back thy image to his idea. The
" agreeable impoſtures of a thouſand dreams
" by night rekindled his ardor. By day
" his ſighs and every thought waited upon
" thy charms.

" It was for thee only, much beloved
" Inès, that thy faithful Don Pedro refuſed
" the heart and hand of princeſſes, exqui-
" ſite

" site in beauty, and eminent in rank. Can
" his royal father counterpoise so violent a
" passion with those murmurs which his
" vassals, eager to see their youthful prince
" wedded to some royal dame, send forth?
" Yes, Alonso's severity decides against the
" tender weakness, now regarded as a crime.
" Unhappy Inès must die. Her death must
" break the slavery in which her beauty
" holds Don Pedro. What fury inspired
" so great a monarch to uplift his hand
" against a life undefended but by tears?
" That sword, so formidable to the Moors,
" abhorred it not being bathed in female
" blood.

" Her cruel enemies now drag poor Inès
" before the king. Her youth, her charms,
" her misfortunes touch him. Heaven-born
" mercy insinuates herself into his breast.
" But the tumultuous cries of his vassals
" awaken his anger afresh. Inès less appre-
" sive of her impending death than of the
" melan-

" melancholy state of solitude in which she
" must leave her prince and the fruits of
" his love, lifts up her eyes bathed with
" tears to heaven; her eyes alone, her fair
" hands were bound, and could not be em-
" ployed in the melancholy office. Then
" turning those fair orbs towards her little
" children, crouding round her, her grief
" is redoubled at the cruel sight. The cold
" hand of affliction benumbs her heart. At
" length breaking silence, she thus bespoke
" the king.

" If it be true that the universe has be-
" held savages and wild beasts, whom na-
" ture teaches cruelty, softened at the af-
" fliction of tender infants, as was the
" foster mother of Nynias, or of the foun-
" ders of Rome; if this be true, O thou,
" who in appearance art human, could hu-
" manity be consistent with the slaughter
" of a wretched damsel, whose only crime
" is to have submitted her heart to the
" youth

" youth who knew how to conquer it?
" O! caſt an eye of pity upon theſe un-
" happy orphans. Let their innocence ſtop
" thy uplifted hand. I ſupplicate thee not
" for my life. My death is wiſhed for. Be
" that wiſh gratified. Yet ſtill, if your
" elemency equals your valor; if you
" know how to ſpare innocence, as you
" can thunder deſtruction in the heat of
" battle upon the brutality of the Moors,
" ſooner than imbrue your hands in my
" blood, baniſh me to ſome unhappy retreat,
" where either frozen Scythia or the burn-
" ing deſerts of Africa reign. Confine me
" where tygers and lions dwell. Among
" them will I ſeek that pity man denies me.
" There attended by my tears and ſighs,
" my heart full of that dear object for which
" I am dragged to puniſhment, there will
" I educate my little ones. The ſight of
" them ſhall be the only conſolation of a
" mother equally tender as unhappy."

Alonſo

Alonso, after having heard the speech of Inès, was rather inclined to treat her with indulgence; but at last he is obliged to yield to the obstinacy of the people, who with unparalleled rigor, says the author, murmur against his mercy; and the principals among them, in a sort of mutiny, draw their swords and murder poor Inès. The words of the author are these.

" Impatient of longer delay their glitter-
" ing swords vibrate in air, to execute of
" themselves, what their mad prepossession
" deems necessary. The blind rage which
" hurries them on, hides from them the
" chastisement soon to break upon their
" heads. One strikes upon that alabaster
" neck, which now no more supports the
" most beautiful visage love ever adored.
" A second buries his steel in that well-
" turned bosom, capable of softening the
" most obdurate heart. Base sanguinary
" butchers, brave only against a tender
" damsel!

" damsel! So Pyrrhus' sword pierced the
" side of the charming Polixena. Yet the
" Grecian's cruelty was less odious. He
" only obeyed his father's spirit. Bright
" torch of day! if horror for the Thyestean
" banquet heretofore forced thee to veil thy
" light under impenetrable clouds, with
" what eye dost thou behold the virtuous
" Inès perish? The crimes of her assassins
" equal that of Atreus. Invert thy course.
" Let the East behold thy setting, for Inès
" dies. Her pale cold mouth pronounces
" her beloved Don Pedro's name mingled
" with the last sigh. As the brilliant co-
" lours of a flower culled by some wanton
" shepherdess languish, so fade the charms,
" the once so enchanting charms of the
" beautiful Inès. Long did the nymphs
" upon Mondego's banks lament her fate,
" but her spectre wandered not unrevenged.
" Her murderers seeing Don Pedro upon
" the throne fly to Castile to evade his
                              " anger.

" anger. But implacable justice pursues
" their steps. The Castilian delivers them
" up. They expire in torments, recom-
" pence worthy of their inhumanity."

LETTER XX.

LISBON, MARCH 12, 1759.

I Will now give a sort of digression of Camouens upon the Portuguese gaining the first sight of the East Indian coast.

"Behold," says he, "intrepid warriors,
"who burn with the desire of honest fame,
"behold the object of your wishes, and ani-
"mate yourselves with new courage. Be-
"fore your eyes lie those happy climes
"which are to crown your fatigues. 'Tis
"to you, O brave posterity of Lusus! (the
"Portuguese), I address myself, who pos-
"sessing but a point upon the globe, yet
"dare affront the greatest dangers, to intro-
"duce the light of truth amongst people
"ignorant

" ignorant of its rays. In such a cause
" weakness retards you not. Valor supplies
" the force you are deficient in. The august
" laws of religion flourish at the expence of
" your blood. But, alas! whilst you, hea-
" ven-assisted, pierce to the utmost confines
" of the world, destroying the worship of
" false deities, the Germans, that haughty
" nation, sovereign of so many provinces,
" abandoned to errors the most detestable,
" in the criminal defence of them are prodi-
" gal of that blood, which with more glory
" might be spent against the Ottomans.

" England, too, tho' mistress of the title of
" ruler of Jerusalem, yet lets that holy city
" groan under Mahometan oppression. Her
" king immersed in softness, enjoys the infa-
" mous luxury of the Assyrians amidst
" northern snows; or if ever he unsheaths
" his sword, it is fatal to the lives of fellow
" Christians.

" But

"But what ought I to say of you, inhabitants of France, whose character was that of candor and equity, but now, hurried on by ambition, you forge chimerical rights to states which belong not to you? If your extensive dominions be not sufficient, why signalize you not your courage upon the banks of Nile and Ciniphus? There would your conquests be legitimate, not so upon your neighbours, who adore the same God. Have you inherited the kingdom of the great Charles and Lewis, but did their justice die with them?

"Thou too, unhappy Italy! land once so respectable! now plunged in vice, I behold thy unhappy offspring enervated by luxury and effeminacy, vile slaves of treasure accumulated with dishonest pains! I behold them leading an inglorious life in the bosom of sloth. Artifice has succeeded to that triumphant valour, which subjected the world to the laws of their ancestors.

" ancestors. But indolence is their slightest
" evil. With cruel divisions they tear in
" pieces the entrails of their bleeding coun-
" try. O miserable inhabitants of Europe!
" what rage animates you against your bre-
" thren? Turn your eyes towards the se-
" pulchre of your holy legislator. Behold it
" in prey to the barbarous descendants of
" Ishmael, always united to attack you, who
" never are so to defend yourselves. Will
" Alecto for ever breathe upon you the spirit
" of discord? Behold, alas! what dangers
" environ you, and how will you escape the
" impending cloud, if you destroy each
" other, while the sons of Mahomet unite
" in your destruction. If riches be your
" aim, the waters of Hermus and Pactolus
" roll over strands of gold. Lydia and As-
" syria enjoy that too precious metal. Afri-
" ca in her bosom conceals abundant veins.
" These climes open an unbounded field to
" your conquests. To amass treasure per-
" form that which you refuse to do for the

interest

"interest of your altars. Your artillery, that tremendous invention, placing thunder in the hands of men, ought to be turned against the walls of Byzantium. Deliver their circumference from the usurpers who occupy it.

"Bid those unjust possessors abandon the peaceful shades of Europe. Bid them return to their Caspian mountains, and the cold inhospitable dens of Scythia. The Greek, the Thracian, the Armenian, demand your assistance. Those nations sinking under the weight of a tyrannic yoke, with tears inform you, that their infants are torn from their breasts, not only to be educated in slavery, but infected with the poison of error and impiety. These are just causes for war. Vie with each other in valor and prudence to chastise Ottoman inhumanity, not to oppress those united to you by the same law.

"But

"But in vain pretend the pious deities of Parnassus to appease the dissensions of Europe. Their voice remains unheard. The furies triumph. Portugal alone treads the paths of real honor."

I will give you one more quotation, which shall be what Camouens says at the conclusion of his poem. He addresses himself to Don Sebastian king of Portugal, his patron, the hero who afterwards fell in Africa, in that famous battle against Muley Moluch, in which both the Moorish and Christian princes were killed; however, the vulgar people in Portugal have a story that Sebastian is not really dead, but only concealed, and that he is to return and restore Portugal to its antient splendor. However, to leave fables and give you the rhapsody of my poet, which is prosaically expressed in what follows.

"Muses no more, my harp is untuned, and my voice begins to fail. 'Tis yours,
"young

" young prince, lord of thefe realms, 'tis
" yours to reanimate my fong. For you
" will I once more invoke the facred nine.
" Afford me but the fubject. Heaven has
" entrufted to your care a nation, whofe loy-
" alty and valor enable you to atchieve any
" undertaking. Your vaffals are ready in
" your fervice to bear the piercing edge of
" hunger, the cruelty of Mars, the injury
" of the feafons, the heats of the burning
" zone, the fnows of either pole, the ftorms
" and monfters of the deep; in a word,
" earth and hell united. Honor them only
" with a favourable regard. Eafe them
" from the yoke of thofe too rigorous laws
" that opprefs them. Let minifters who
" join undoubted probity to long experience
" be your advifers. Be thofe alfo confined
" to the foot of the altars, whofe duty it is
" to fee their worfhip duly performed, nor
" let them, precipitated by vain ambition,
" trouble your people by attempting to go-
" vern them. The duty of priefts is to lift

"up their hands to your celestial master,
"imploring in your favor his eternal wis-
"dom. With them other occupations are
"criminal. In a word, young prince, reign
"by yourself; nor let Italy, Germany,
"France or England, heretofore the admi-
"rers of Portugal, let them not say that
"her glory is obscured, or that her sons are
"become slaves. Then will I touch again
"the sounding lyre to celebrate thy fame,
"and whilst haughty Atlas trembles in be-
"holding thee, while the affrighted plains
"of Ampelusia bear witness to the flight of
"the warriors of Marocco and Tarudant,
"will I extend thy praises to the end of the
"globe. The universal globe, seized with
"awe and affection, shall confess in my
"prince a second Alexander, who need not
"envy the happiness of Achilles."

It is with this high-flown compliment to himself that our poet ends his work, the

meaning

meaning of which you know is alluding to Alexander's having said that he envied Achilles in nothing, but in having Homer to record his actions. A bold stroke in Camouens to equal himself to Homer at the same time he compares Don Sebastian to Alexander. From these few passages you may perhaps be able to form some little, but imperfect idea of that author. You may wonder what I have been quoting in this and my former paper has to do for the most part with a voyage to India. What I gave you in the foregoing was taken out of the Episode, in which he gives some description of Europe to the king of Melinda, but more especially of the affairs of Portugal; and as for this last quotation, you see it is merely an apostrophe to the king for the conclusion of his poem. I think for a Roman catholic country he speaks very freely of the priests. It must be rather an affecting passage to the Portuguese in the
present

present state of things. The late affair of the jesuits comes too *apropos* to what he says about church ambition not to be taken notice of.

LETTER XXI.

LISBON, MARCH 17, 1759.

A Dark mift ftill hanging over the affairs of the jefuits, and as the misfortunes of our fellow countrymen always intereft us, I fhall therefore, without farther preamble, fend you an account of the cataftrophe of the late James Read, Efq. conful general of Barbary.

Mr. Read, late of Gibraltar, was in the month of July, 1757, appointed conful general to the king of Marocco. Mr. Pitt fent him out his commiffion by a meffenger on purpofe, who arrived at Gibraltar the laft day of September; and upon the twelfth of October he embarked for Sallee, on board the Syren Frigate. He foon got from Sallee to Marocco, where the young prince Sidi Mahomet refided, who, by the confent of his father Muley Abdallah then living, held the reins of government, and tranfacted all affairs with foreign powers. It was this young prince that had demanded a conful, and defired to have a peace renewed with the Englifh.

While Mr. Read was at Marocco, the king Abdallah died, and Sidi Mahomet his fon fucceeded without oppofition to the throne, which he ftill continues to enjoy.

Mr. Read was furprized to find that he was received with great coolnefs, and even with a kind of contempt. Nor did Sidi Mahomet accept more gracioufly the prefents that Mr. Read had brought him, but feemed to defpife them as of little value, tho' they coft above £600; and he had received another which was very handfome, about four months before, and had been fent out from England

England on purpofe. Some attribute the reafon of this bad treatment and coolnefs to our having neglected the fon too much during the life of his father; but it feems in part to have been owing to the inftigation of the French intereft in thofe countries, who endeavoured to reprefent every thing concerning us in the worft light. By the beginning, however, of December, Mr. Read had adjufted matters with him in the beft manner poffible; tho', indeed, all he had obtained was a truce for a twelvemonth, during which interval he was to folicit a letter from our king himfelf, in anfwer to the many exorbitant demands which the Moorifh fovereign made. He had been affronted at Mr. Pitt's only writing himfelf, and faid he expected a letter from the king's own hand, and not from that of his fecretaries; an office which the Moors do not feem much to underftand. Upon thefe terms they parted, and Mr. Read was on his way back to Gibraltar, and had now got as far as Sallee,

when

when an unlucky, tho' deferved accident, happened to one of the cruizers of the Moorifh king. She fell in with the fame frigate which had brought Mr. Read to Sallee, in her return from thence. The Moorifh veffel miftaking her for a merchant fhip, (as the Syren is fmall,) hoped eafily to make her a prey; and difcharged a broadfide, which was followed with an attempt to board. But the Syren beftirring herfelf, drove the cruizer on fhore upon the Barbary coaft, near Cape Spartel, where fhe perifhed. The news of this accident was foon fpread abroad, and the king immediately fent after Mr. Read, with orders to ftop him at Sallee, and demand fatisfaction for the lofs of his fhip. About the fame time Mr. Read received a letter from admiral Ofborne, who then commanded the Mediterranean fleet, informing him of the whole tranfaction. In order to anticipate any demand on the part of the Moorifh king, he defired Mr. Read to infift upon

M   fatisfaction

satisfaction for the affront offered to our flag in firing upon an English vessel with British colours flying. Mr. Read acted as admiral Osborne had told him, and appeared astonished when the king made his complaints to him upon that subject. But Sidi Mahomet persisted in asserting that his cruizer had been unjustly destroyed, and demanded 20000 ducats, about £6000. sterling, as an equivalent. The consul upon refusal of this was confined to a close room at Sallee. However, he was kept there but a few hours, and was then sent back a prisoner to his house, which was surrounded by a detachment of guards.

He continued in this state till the king came to Fez, in a tour he was making thro' his new dominions. He here ordered Mr. Read to be brought up to him from Sallee, in order to determine something concerning their difference. The consul arrived at Fez the 29th of January, 1758, and the day after

after wrote letters to his friends at Gibraltar, which fhew he was in good health and fpirits. However, he little knew how bufy his enemies in Barbary were, and that every contrivance was putting in practice to fet the king againft him. Upon his arrival at Fez he was again befet with guards, and during feveral days had frequent meffages fent him by the king, who ftill demanded fatisfaction, which Mr. Read peremptorily refufed.

But as my hiftory proves rather long, the remainder of it muft be deferred to my next paper.

LETTER XXII.

LISBON, MARCH 14, 1759.

On the 16th of February, 1758, Mr. Read and Mr. Grosvenor, a lieutenant of marines belonging to the Syren frigate, who had accompanied the consul upon this expedition, were both ordered to appear before the king. In this audience he broke out into exclamations and revilings against the English in general, and Mr. Read in particular, with many opprobrious terms, threatening to torture and burn him if he did not grant his demands with regard to the ship. This the consul steadily refused to do as unjust, and bore the king's treatment with much composure of mind, which irritated the Barbarian monarch's pride to that degree as made him order his guards to

seize

seize upon Mr. Read and drag him to a dungeon. Before they carried him down they buffeted him according to the Moorish custom, and then drove him headlong into it with kicks and cuffs. It was here, indeed, Mr. Read's composure of mind abandoned him. His passions broke loose, and wrought him into a rage, which agitated his spirits so violently, that it quite unhinged him, if I may be allowed the expression, and left him in a dejection of mind which he never got the better of. He was detained about three hours in this dungeon, and when relieved was threatened with worse usage, if he did not submit to the king's demand.

Upon the 17th the king sent several messages to Mr. Read and the English with him, accompanying them every time with different menaces. The threats, however, of this day ended in a determination to pronounce them slaves, and set them to work with the Portuguese and Spaniards in captivity.

Upon this treatment Mr. Read appeared very dejected, but full of resentment, without knowing how to unburden himself. It was upon this day that he sat down to write some letters to his friends, which testify the great extremities to which he was driven by these Barbarians, and that he had an intention of destroying himself.

In the mean time he received several fresh threats from the king, who insisted sometimes upon one thing and then upon another, without observing any rule or measure in his words or actions.

The next morning, the 18th of February, the king sent his attendants to Mr. Read with orders to carry him and all his companions away as slaves. Mr. Grosvenor was the first that was conducted out of the house to be made a favorite slave of the king's and to be always near his person. Mr. Read and his domestics were to follow, but they were
sentenced

sentenced to remain among the working slaves. Mr. Read was hardly got beyond the door of his apartment when he begged to return into it for something he had left, which the guards allowed him. As soon as he was entered, he locked the door after him, and in about a minute's time the report of a pistol was heard. His servants were much alarmed, and one of them ran after Mr. Grosvenor who had not been conducted very far from the house. Having got leave to return he knocked for some time at the door, but no reply followed from within. It was then agreed to break it open, which was immediately done, and Mr. Read was found dead upon the floor.

Upon having shut the door he had recourse to his pocket pistols, one of which he took in each hand, and applying that in his right to his head, fired it. As he stood by the bedside, his head fell first upon the sheets and left a bloody mark, but his knees, I imagine,

gine, failing by degrees, dragged him down upon the floor, where he lay with his legs under the bed. Thus ended the unfortunate Mr. Read. The king was said to appear astonished at the news, but it does not seem to have much influenced his future conduct. On the contrary he has made slaves of all our men who were wrecked on his coast about three months and a half ago in the Litchfield and two other vessels, a frigate of thirty-six guns, and an ammunition ship, that were going with our fleet to the reduction of Gorée.

He then sent to the governor of Gibraltar to acquaint him that he considered the truce between him and the English as at an end, and that if they wanted their men they must be ransomed. Captain Barton, the captain of the Litchfield *, with the rest who
escaped

---

* It may not, perhaps, be disagreeable to the reader, especially as there will be some little more hereafter
of

escaped the fury of the seas, are now at Marocco, and we are anxious to know how our government of Barbary affairs, if I subjoin the following account of the loss of this ship and the behaviour of the Moors to our people, written by James Southerland, lieutenant on board the Litchfield.

" The Litchfield left Ireland the 11th of November 1758, in company with several other men of war and transports under the command of commodore Keppel, and intended for the reduction of Gorée. The wind proved mostly fair till the 22d of November, then kept pretty constant from south-east to south-west, and our voyage was prosperous till the 28th. On which day at eight in the evening I took charge of the watch, when the weather turned out very squally with rain. We were then under our courses and main top sail. At nine it was exceedingly dark with much lightning, the wind varying from south-west to north-west. At half an hour past nine there was an extreme hard squall. Captain Barton then came upon deck and stayed till ten, leaving orders to keep sight of the commodore, and to make what sail the weather would permit. We saw the commodore at eleven bearing south, but the squalls encreasing, at twelve o'clock we were obliged to hand the main top sail under our courses.

" At

government will proceed with regard to them. Indeed I flatter myself that this treatment

"At one o'clock in the morning, November 29th, I left the deck in charge of the firſt lieutenant, the light which we took to be the commodore's bearing ſouth right a-head, the wind weſt-ſouth-weſt blowing very hard. I was awakened at ſix in the morning by a great ſhock and a confuſed noiſe of the men on deck. I ran to ſee what was the matter, thinking that ſome ſhip was fallen foul of us, as I had no thoughts of land being near us at the time, being then, by my own reckoning and that of every perſon in the ſhip, at leaſt 35 leagues diſtance from it. But before I could reach the quarter deck, I was ſenſibly convinced of our diſmal ſituation, by the ſhip's giving a great ſtroke againſt the ground, and the ſeas breaking all over us. Juſt after this I could perceive the land, which appeared to be rocky, rugged, and uneven, and was about two cables length from us. The ſhip lying with her broad-ſide to windward the ſea broke entirely over her. The maſts ſoon went overboard with very little aſſiſtance, and ſome men were carried off with them. It is impoſſible for any perſon but a ſufferer to feel our diſtreſs at this time. The maſts, yards and ſails were hanging along ſide in a confuſed heap, the ſhip was beating violently upon the rocks, and the waves were curling up to a prodigious

treatment will draw upon the Moors the vengeance due to them. Not but that a war with

digious height, then dashing down with such force as if they would immediately have split the ship to pieces, which indeed we every moment expected. Providence, however, favored us greatly, for some of the large waves breaking without us, the remainder of their force came against our our starboard quarter, and the anchors, which we cut away as soon as we struck, now assisted us in bringing the ship's head towards the sea. This gave us a glimpse of prolonging life, perhaps, a few hours, which was all at that time we could expect, when we beheld the rugged rocks, and thought every moment to be torn asunder by the fierce roaring surf. However, our scattered senses now recovered a little, and we saw it necessary to get every thing we could over to the starboard side, to prevent the ship from heeling off and exposing the deck again to the sea; and the waves for the most part breaking forward, we catched the opportunity, and got most of the starboard guns overboard, with what else we could come at. Some of the people, contrary to advice, were very earnest to get out the boats, however after much entreaty, notwithstanding the prospect of a most terrible sea, one of the boats was launched and eight of the best men jumped into her. But although at this time the sea was

rather

with such a barbarous race of people is disagreeable, as much may be lost, but nothing gained;

rather abated, she had hardly got to the ship's stern than she was instantly whirled to the bottom and every person in her perished. The rest of the boats were soon dashed to pieces upon deck. We then made a raft with the davit capstain bars and some boards, which being done, nothing remained but to wait with resignation for the assistance of Divine Providence. The ship was so soon filled with water, that we had no time to get any provision up. The quarter deck and poop were now the only places we could stand on with any security, the waves being mostly spent by the time they reached us, owing to the fore part of the ship breaking them. At four in the afternoon, perceiving the sea to be much abated, as it was almost low water I was thinking to make an attempt of swimming on shore, as we had reason to imagine the ship would not withstand the violence of the next flood, for she now began to drop to pieces very fast. One of the people attempted it and got safe to land. There were numbers of Moors upon the rocks who seemed ready to take hold of any one, and beckoned much for us to come on shore. This at first we took for kindness, but they soon undeceived us, for self interest was their only view, as they had not the humanity to assist any body that was entirely naked,

gained; however, in my opinion, the honor of our country demands some satisfaction.

With

naked, but would fly to them who had any thing about them and strip them before they were quite out of the water, wrangling among themselves about the plunder. In the mean time the poor man was left to crawl up the rocks if he was able, if not it was a matter of indifference. However the second lieutenant and myself with about sixty-five others got on shore before dark, but were for some time uncertain whether we had not made a wrong choice, for here we were left exposed to the weather upon the cold sand. To keep ourselves from perishing we were obliged to go down to the shore and bring up pieces of our wreck to make a fire. If we happened to pick up a shirt or handkerchief, and did not give it up to the Moors at the first demand, the next thing was a dagger offered to our breast. They allowed us, however, a piece of an old sail, which they did not think worth carrying off, and of this we made two tents and crouded ourselves into them, every one sitting between the others legs to preserve warmth and make room. In this uneasy situation, continually bewailing ourselves and our poor shipmates upon the wreck, we passed a most tedious rainy blowing night, without so much as a drop of water to refresh us, except what we catched through our sail-cloth coverings.

" November

With regard to the authenticity of what I have related, I had it from an account written

"November 30th. Fresh gales, hard squalls, and rain. At six in the morning we went down with a number of our men to assist our shipmates in coming on shore, and found the ship had been greatly shattered in the night. It being now low water, many attempted to swim to land. Some got safe, others perished. The people on board got the raft into the water, and about fifteen men upon it; but they were no sooner put off from the wreck than it quite overturned. Most part of the men recovered it again, but were hardly on before it was overturned a second time. There were only three or four that got hold of it a third time, the rest perished. During this interval a good swimmer brought a rope on shore with much difficulty, which I had the good fortune (by running hastily over the sharp rocks into the water,) to catch hold of, just as he was quite spent, and had thoughts of quitting it. Some people coming to my assistance, we pulled a large rope on shore with that, and made it fast round a rock. This we found gave great spirits to the poor souls upon the wreck; for as it was stretched tight from the upper part of the stern, it made an easy descent to any who had art enough to walk or slide upon a rope, with another above to hold by.

written by a merchant of Gibraltar, who was partner to Mr. Read. This gentleman endeavours

by. They continued coming by the rope till about eleven o'clock, tho' many were wafhed off by the impetuofity of the furf, and loft. High water coming on raifed the furf ftill more, and prevented others from venturing at this time, as the ropes could be of no further ufe. We then retired from the rocks, and hunger prevailing, went about broiling fome of the drowned turkeys, &c. which, with fome flower baked upon the fire, made our firft meal upon this barbarous coaft. We found a well of frefh water about half a mile off, which very much rejoiced us. But we had hardly finifhed this coarfe repaft, than the Moors (who were now grown very numerous,) drove us every one down to the rocks; beating us if we lingered, tho' fome were hardly able to crawl, to bring up empty bound cafks, pieces of the wreck which had moft iron about them, and other things. About three o'clock in the afternoon we made another meal on our drowned poultry, and finding this was the beft fare we were likely to have, fome were ordered to fave all they could pick up upon the fhore, others to raife a larger tent, and the reft were fent down to the rocks to look for people coming on fhore. The furf greatly increafing with the flood, and breaking upon

the

endeavours to excuse his laying violent hands upon himself by divers reasons; but as the facts

the fore part of the ship, she was now divided into three pieces. The fore part was turned keel up, and the middle part was soon dashed into a thousand bits. The fore part of the poop fell likewise at this time, and about thirty men with it, eight of whom got safe to shore with our help, but so bruised, that we despaired of their recovery. Now was to be seen a most melancholy prospect. Nothing but the after part of the poop remained above water, with a very small part of the other decks, on which our captain, and about one hundred and thirty more remained, expecting every wave to be their last; for the wreck seemed as if it was going instantly to throw them all to the bottom, and overset upon them. Every shock threw some off, few or none of them came on shore alive. During this distress the Moors laughed very loud, and seemed much diverted when a wave larger than common threatened our poor tottering countrymen with destruction. Between four and five o'clock the sea was much decreased with the ebb. The rope being still secure, they began to venture upon it. About five we beckoned as much as possible for the captain to come upon the rope, as this seemed to be as good an opportunity as any we had seen, and many

came

facts conclude here, I shall leave you to make the determination upon them your own judgment suggests.

LET-

came safe with our assistance. Some told us that the captain was determined to stay till all the men had made the best of their way to land, or, at least, had quitted the wreck; which bravery of his, tho' we could not but admire, we could not but deplore. However, we still continued to beckon for him, and just before it was dark we saw him come upon the rope. He was close followed by a good able seaman, who did all he could to keep up his spirits, and assist him. As he could not swim, and had been so long without any refreshment, with the surf hurling him violently along, he was no longer able to resist the force of the waves, and had unavoidably perished, if a wave had not thrown him within reach of our ropes, which he had barely the sense left to catch hold of. We pulled him up, when after resting a little time upon the rocks, he came to himself, and walked up to the tent; desiring us still to assist the people in coming on shore. The Moors wanted to have stript him, tho' he had nothing on but a plain waistcoat and breeches, if we had not shewn a little spirit on this occasion, and opposed them; upon which they thought proper to desist. The people

continued

LETTER XXIII.

LISBON, MARCH 27, 1759.

I promised you some further account of the affair of the jesuits in these countries. But as a deep cloud seems still to overwhelm the whole

continued to come on shore pretty fast, tho' many perished in the attempt, but they plainly saw their case was desperate, as the wreck must inevitably fall to pieces with the next flood. The Moors growing tired with waiting for so little plunder, would not let us stay after them upon the rocks, but drove us all up. I then, with the captain's approbation, went and made humble petition by signs to the basha or commander, who was in his tent with many other Moors, dividing the valuable spoil. He understood me at last, and gave us leave to go down, sending some Moors with us. We carried fire brands along with us to let the poor wretches upon the wreck see we were still there ready to assist them. I dare say several perished while

whole affair, I will wait another week in hopes of its diffipating. With regard to the nobles

while we were gone, for want of our help; for we had been but a few minutes upon the rocks when one came very near to us before we faw him. And this was frequently a circumftance of as much horror as any we met with; for juft as we had been able to perceive them, they have been wafhed from the rope, and dafhed to death againft the rocks clofe by us. About nine at night, finding no more would venture upon the rope, as the furf was greatly increafed, we retired to our tent with hearts full of forrow; leaving, by the laft man's account, between thirty and forty fouls upon deck. We now thought of ftowing every body into the tent, and began by fixing the captain in the middle. We then made every perfon lie down upon their fides, as taking up lefs room than upon their backs. But after all many enjoyed eafier lodgings in empty cafks.

" December 1ft, moderate and fair weather. In the morning the wreck was all to pieces upon the rocks, and the fhore was quite covered with lumber. The people upon the wreck all perifhed about one in the morning, as we learnt from one who was toffed up and down for near

two

nobles I think there is nothing more to add. Some of them, indeed, have been relegated to

two hours upon a piece of it, and at laſt thrown upon the rocks ſenſeleſs; but he recovered, and got to the tent by day light, tho' greatly bruiſed.

" The Moors were very buſy in picking up every thing of value, but would not ſuffer us to take the leaſt trifle, except pork, flower and liquor: of all which we ſecured as much as we could in the tent. In the mean time, others were enlarging and raiſing a ſecond. Some were were trying to make bread, and others cleaning the drowned ſtock. At one in the afternoon we called a muſter, and placing the men all in rank and file, we found our number to be two hundred and twenty. A hundred and thirty were drowned; among which number was the firſt lieutenant, the captain of marines, his lieutenant, the purſer, gunner, carpenter, and three midſhipmen. We now returned public thanks to Almighty God for our deliverance.

" December 2d, moderate and fair weather. At five in the morning we found George Allen, a marine, dead cloſe by the tents, which we ſuppoſe was by drinking brandy

to Angola, and other parts of the Portuguese dominions; and the remainder are still in

brandy among the rocks, as several had got drunk that way, tho' we used what means we could to prevent it. There were two men whipt by captain Barton's orders, for their insolence, which was highly necessary, both to convince the Moors and our own men, that they were still under our command. We subsisted entirely upon the drowned stock, with a little salt pork to relish it, and the flower made into cakes. We issued these provisions regularly and sparingly, not knowing at present whether we should have any thing from the Moors or no; as they still continued to be very troublesome, and wanted to rob us of the canvas which covered our tent. Their basha seemed to take our part, but at the same time winked at their villainy, and shared in the plunder. He employed us in saving all the iron we could from the pieces of the wreck. At two in the afternoon there arrived a black servant, sent by one Mr. Butler at Saffy, (a town about thirty miles off,) to enquire into our condition, and give us assistance. The captain wrote him a letter, the man having brought us pens, ink and paper: and the finding there was one offered us help, greatly raised our drooping spirits.

"Decem-

in prifon. You tell me you are wondering how the people here live without houfes. It is true

"December 3d Moderate weather, fometimes raining. In the morning we affembled the people, and read prayers of thankfgiving. In the afternoon a letter came from Mr Butler, with fome bread, and a few other neceffaries. We heard, likewife, that one of the tranfports and a bomb tender were wrecked about three leagues to the northward of us, and a great many men faved.

"December 4th. Moderate weather. The people were employed in picking up pieces of fail cloth, and what elfe the Moors would permit them. We diftributed the people into meffes, and ferved the neceffaries we received the day before. They had bread and the flefh of the drowned ftock. In the afternoon we had another letter from Mr. Butler, who is factor to the Danifh African company, and himfelf a Dane. We had likewife another letter at the fame time from one Mr. Andrews, an Irifh gentleman, a merchant at Saffy. The Moors were not fo troublefome as before; moft of them going off with what they had got.

"December 5th. Squally weather, with rain. As the drowned ftock was all expended, the people were employed

true the earthquake and fire destroyed most of them; some, however, were so little damaged

ed at low water in gathering muscles. At ten in the morning Mr. Andrews arrived, and brought a French surgeon with him, and some medicines and plaisters: of which many of the bruised men stood in very great need. Thomas Tompion, seaman, died in the afternoon, by his bruises mortifying. Several men were employed in rolling casks of water from the well.

" December 6th. Squally, rainy weather. We served one of this country blankets to every two men, and pampooses (a sort of slippers,) to those who were most in need of them. These supplies were brought by Mr. Andrews. The people now were forced to live upon muscles and bread, as the Moors had deceived us, and not returned, tho' they promised to supply us with cattle.

" December 7th. Dirty squally weather, with rain. The people were employed in gathering muscles and limpets. The Moors began to be a little civil, for fear the emperor should punish them for their cruel usage. In the afternoon a messenger arrived from the emperor, who was at Sallee, with orders in general to the people to supply

naged as to be eafily repaired and rendered habitable. They have likewife run up temporary

ply us with provifions. Accordingly, they brought fome poor bullocks and lean fheep, which Mr. Andrews purchafed for us. But at this time we had no pots to make broth in, and the cattle were fcarce fit for any thing elfe.

" December 8th. Squally weather, with heavy rain. The people were ferved this morning with mutton and bread, and employed in rolling water from the well.

" December 9th. Little wind, with fhowers of rain. In the morning we faw feveral dead bodies caft up by the fea upon the rocks. The people employed in bringing up the oak timber, &c. &c. from the fea fide, as the emperor had fent orders to fave whatever might be of ufe to his cruizers.

" December 10th. Light airs, and fair weather. In the morning we got every thing ready to march to Marocco; the emperor having fent orders to that purpofe, with camels to carry the lame and baggage. At nine we fet out with about thirty camels, having got all our liquor with us, divided into hogfheads for the conveniency of carriage.

porary edifices, besides an immense quantity of barracks, or huts as we might call them in

carriage. At noon we joined the crews of the other two transports, which had been wrecked as well as ourselves. Every person was then mounted upon camels, except the captain, who was furnished with a horse. We never stopt till seven in the evening, when they procured us only two tents, which would not hold one third of the men; so that most of them lay exposed to the dew, which was heavy and very cold.

" We now found our whole number to be three hundred and twenty eight, including officers, men and boys: with three women and a child, which one of them brought on shore, holding it by its cloaths in her teeth.

" December 11th. Fair pleasant weather. We now continued our journey in the morning, attended by a number of Moors on horseback. The alcaide who had the conducting of us provided several of the officers with horses. We did not travel straight towards Marocco, being informed we must meet the emperor at Sailee. At six in the evening we came to our resting place for the night, and were furnished with tents sufficient to cover all the men.

We

in England. The reason of these buildings being erected out of the town is owing, as I think

We found our conductors seldom stopped from sun-rise to sun-set; that being the custom of the country, with which we were obliged to comply.

" December 12th. Fair weather. At five in the morning we set out as before, and at two in the afternoon saw the emperor's cavalcade at a distance. At three a relation of the emperor's, named Muley Adriffe came to us, and told the captain it was the emperor's orders he should that instant write a letter to our governor at Gibraltar, to send to his Britannic majesty, to know whether he would settle a peace with him or no. Captain Barton sat down directly upon the grass and wrote a letter, which he gave to Muley Adriffe, who went and rejoined the emperor. At six in the evening we came to our resting place for the night, and were well furnished with tents, tho' very little provision.

" December 13th. Pleasant weather. We continued here till the men were a little refreshed, of which they stood much in need. They brought us more provisions than the day before. This morning lieutenant Harrison,

commanding

think I have already mentioned, to no person being allowed to build quite on fresh

within

commanding officer of the soldiers belonging to lord Forbes' regiment, died suddenly in the tent. In the evening, while we were burying him, the inhuman Moors disturbed us by throwing stones and mocking us.

" December 14th. Pleasant weather. Our men recovered greatly with the rest we had here. They were furnished with earthen pots to make broth in.

" December 15th. The people were mostly employed in cooking, as we were now pretty well supplied with beef. This morning we found the Moors had opened lieutenant Harrison's grave, and stript the cloaths from off him.

" December 16th. Fair weather. We continued our journey as before. At five in the afternoon we came to our resting place, pitched our tents, and served the people with provisions. Here some of the country Moors used our people ill as they were taking water from a brook. The Moors would always spit in the vessel before they would let them take any away. Some of us upon

this

within it; as all the streets are to be formed according to a certain plan, which the court has

this went down to inquire into it, but were saluted with a shower of stones. We run in upon them, beat them pretty soundly, put them to flight, and brought away one who thought to defend himself with a long knife. This fellow was severely punished by the alcaide who had the conducting of us.

" December 17th. Fair weather. In the the morning we gave the people a dram each, as had been usual, and continued our journey. At four in the afternoon we came to our resting place for the night. After some difficulty we got tents, and a proper supply of provisions.

" December 18th. Fair weather. This morning we proceeded on our journey as before, and at three in the afternoon came to the city of Marocco, without having seen one dwelling house in the whole way. We here were insulted by the rabble as we passed. At five o'clock we were carried before the emperor, surrounded by five or six hundred of his guards. He was on horseback before his palace gate, that being the place where he distributed justice to his people. He told captain Barton that he

has not yet issued out, nor does it seem at all certain when it will be settled.

In

he was neither at peace or war with England, and that he would detain us till an ambassador came from thence to settle a firm peace. The captain then desired that we might not be used as slaves. He replied hastily, that we should be taken care of. Then we were directly thrust out of his presence, and conveyed to two old ruined houses, where we were shut up all night amidst dirt and innumerable vermin of several sorts. Mr. Butler, whom I mentioned before, being here upon business, came and assisted us, and procured liberty for the captain to go home with him to his lodgings. He likewise sent some blankets for the officers, with which we made a shift to pass the night pretty comfortably, as we were much tired and fatigued.

" December 19th. Cloudy weather, blowing fresh, with rain. This morning we found our centry was taken off, so that the people had liberty to go out. They sent us moreover some bread, and towards evening some beef, but we had no conveniencies as yet to dress it, and the people were all day employed in cleaning out the rubbish and destroying the vermin as well as they could.

" Decem-

In the mean time spring is approaching with hasty steps in these countries, and I shall shortly be setting out for Spain.

LET-

"December 20th. Little wind and rain. This morning some of our baggage was brought to us, with the necessaries we had upon the road. Our baggage had been rummaged, and the captain's trunk robbed of nineteen ducats, several rings, and silver buckles, a watch and other things, mostly belonging to the officers, and which we had with difficulty saved from the wreck. Mr. Butler and his partner Mr. Dekon did every think in their power to assist us. The people had now pots to boil their victuals, and were in no want of bread.

"December 21st. Cloudy weather with rain at times. This day the emperor sent money to the captain to support his men, at a blanqueen a day each, or two pence sterling. But as that was too little, captain Barton got money of Mr. Butler to make it up two blanqueens, or four pence sterling, which he managed himself to the best advantage, allowing them one pound of beef each, with broth, and one pound of bread each every day. At nine this morning the emperor sent for the captain and every officer to appear before him. We immediately repaired to his

palace,

LETTER XXIV.

LISBON, APRIL 1, 1759.

I Will now, tho' it is still possible to do it but lamely, give you what I know concerning

palace, where we remained waiting in an outer yard two hours. In the mean time he was diverting himself in seeing a clumsy Dutch boat rowed along by four of our petty officers. About noon we were called and placed in a line about thirty yards before him. He was seated in a chair by the side of a pond, with only two of the chief alcaides with him. When he had viewed us some time, he ordered the captain to come forward, and after asking him a good many questions concerning our navy, and where our squadron was going, we were also called before him by two or three at a time, as we stood according to our rank. He asked most of us some very insignificant questions, and took some to be Portuguese, because they had black hair, and others to be Swedes because they had white

ing the jefuits, for I believe it is in vain to expect things will become clearer at prefent.

You white hair, judging none of us to be right Englifh, except the captain, the fecond lieutenant, the enfign of marines and myfelf. But we affured him we were all Englifh, fo that crying *bon*, he gave a nod for our departure. To this we returned a very low bow, and were glad to get our old ruined manfion again. Our number of officers at this time was thirty from higheft to loweft.

"December 22d. Fair weather. Captain Barton provided the people with ftuffs for frocks and troufers, and mats and pillows to lay upon, with every other neceffary that could be got. They were all employed in making themfelves clothes in the beft manner they could.

"December 23d. This morning the emperor fent a meffage to the captain, with orders, if any of his men fhould be guilty of a crime, to punifh them in the fame manner as if they were on board his fhip. But fuppofing they fhould quarrel with the Moors, they muft ftand to the Moorifh laws, which are very fevere againft Chriftians. This day Henry Nicholas was punifhed for getting drunk and abufing his officers.

" De-

You remember what a noife the affairs of that fociety in America made in Europe. When Spain

" December 24th. The people were very well fatisfied with their provifions. This being Sunday we affembled them all and read prayers as if we had been on board. It is to be obferved we had but one bible amongft us all, which was a prefent from Mr. Andrews before mentioned, and tho' we had no clergyman, captain Barton never omitted a fingle Sunday to have fervice performed, either by the fecond lieutenant or myfelf.

" December 25th. Being Chriftmas day, prayers were read to the people as ufual in the church of England. The captain received a prefent of fome tea and loaves of fugar from one of the queens, whofe grandfather had been an Englifh renegado.

" December 26th. This afternoon we heard the difagreeable news, that the emperor would oblige all the Englifh to work, the fame as the other Chriftian flaves, except the officers that were before him on the 21ft inftant.

" December 27th. Cloudy weather with rain. At feven this morning an alcaide came and ordered the people all

Spain had agreed with Portugal to exchange the extensive country of Paraguai against their

all out to work, except those that were sick, and by intercession eight were allowed to stay at home every day as cooks for the others. This they took by turns throughout the whole number. They returned at four in the afternoon. Some had been employed in carrying wood, some in turning up the ground with hoes, and others in picking weeds in the emperor's gardens.

" December 28th. Cloudy weather. All the people went to work as soon as they could see. They were allowed to sit down an hour and a half in the middle of the day, but had many a stroke from their drivers, tho' they were doing their utmost to deserve better usage. Captain Barton was striving all that was in his power to get this remedied, which by the assistance of a friend of ours, one Juan Arbona, we were in hopes of doing. This person had been eight years in Africa, and was taken under English colours, notwithstanding he had a pass signed by general Blakeney at Minorca. The emperor had kept him for two or three years past near his own person, and put much confidence in him. At four in the afternoon the people returned. Two of the marines had a hundred

bastinadoes

their settlement of Nueva Colonia, the jesuits who had originally been sent thither as missionaries,

bastinadoes each, for behaving in a disrespectful manner while the emperor was looking at their work.

" December 29th. Cloudy weather. The people went to work as before. They were now allowed a hot breakfast of a sort of porridge sweetened with honey before they set out. Their work was sometimes to till the ground, at other times to carry wood or stone for building, and such other things as slaves are commonly employed in.

" December 30th, captain Barton received a kind letter from the emperor, with his leave to ride out or take a walk in his gardens with any of his officers.

" As we were now got into a settled way, and as most of the same things daily revolved, I shall only remark any extraordinary occurrences.

" About the beginning of February two soldiers died, within a few days of each other. The emperor enquiring the reason of this, was told by Juan Arbona, that it was occasioned by their catching cold for want of cloaths.

missionaries, defended the former, as they do still, against the united forces of Spain and

Upon this he was directly ordered to give every English slave as much white linen as would make him two shirts.

" Upon the 22d of March a Spaniard having some words with a Moor, who had first used him ill, was carried before the emperor, who being in a bad humour that day, ordered the poor fellow to be knocked on the head directly with a hoe, and the dead body to be exposed for two days afterwards. During this time the Moors and Jews shewed their disposition by dashing the body to pieces with stones as they passed. We now received letters from Gibraltar which gave us hopes of speedy relief. Our men was not so healthy as at first, some having got the flux and others fevers.

" On the 26th of May we received a letter from the governor of Gibraltar, with an offer of one hundred and seventy thousand dollars as a present to the emperor for our freedom. He seemed very well pleased with this, and promised to send immediately for the ambassador at Gibraltar, who was appointed to transact these affairs.

" June 15th, a courier, by name Toledano, a Jew, set out with the emperor's letters to the ambassador.

" The

and Portugal, refusing to yield it up to either, and some of them became generals to the

"The 2d of July the emperor set out from Marocco with an army of six thousand men, which, by report, was soon to be augmented to thirty thousand. He went to subdue some part of his dominions that would not acknowledge his sovereignty.

"About the 10th, seventy mens heads were sent from the camp, and placed against one of the great gates of the city, besides several alive, who were capitally punished. The emperor about four or five days journey from Marocco had some smart skirmishes.

"It was now the middle of September, when we were assured of the long expected arrival of our ambassador at Sallee with two of his majesty's ships, the Guernsey and Thetis. The emperor was acquainted at his camp with the money for our redemption being on board; but elated with his success by land and sea, and having nothing to fear till the next spring, he only trifled with us by making extravagant demands. Our ambassador at last very prudently left the coast, having lost two anchors in Sallee road.

the Indians, who blindly followed perfons that had already enflaved their confciences, and

" The latter end of September the emperor returned to Marocco after having finifhed his campaign fuccefsfully.

" He at laft, tho' not before the beginning of February, refolved to fend Toledano a third time to Gibraltar (he had fent him a fecond time the preceding October). He ordered him, as his final determination, to accept of two hundred thoufand dollars for all the Englifh fubjects in his dominions, and twenty-five thoufand dollars for all other pretenfions, which terms were agreed to by the governor.

" In confequence of this, on the 11th of April our men left off going to work, and on the 12th in the evening the emperor fent for captain Barton, the fecond lieutenant and myfelf, and told us we were going next morning, and that he would make peace with our nation if they were willing, if not he did not care. He then gave a nod for our departure, which we moft chearfully accepted with a very low bow and went away.

" Accordingly next morning, being all ready before fun-rife, we waited till nine o'clock for the mules and

camels•

and whom they deemed faints. This caufed the firft noife about them in Europe, and pope Benedict XIV. nominated cardinal Saldania, patriarch of Lifbon, reformer and vifitor of this affair with the moft ample powers. The cardinal fufpended the jefuits from preaching and confeffing, however, I fuppofe for political reafons, they were ac-

camels. When all were come, we proceeded upon our journey attended by a bafha and one hundred foldiers on horfe-back. Captain Barton was now confulted how faft he chofe to travel and when to ftop. In the evening we pitched our tents in the form of an exact oval, the captain's clofing one end and ours the other.

" We got to Sallee the 22d of April, and pitched our tents in an old caftle, from whence we had the happinefs once again to fee our royal mafter's fhips ready to receive us. But when we viewed the bar of the harbour covered with a large roaring furf, we began to think our embarkation would probably prove tedious, which accordingly happened. At laft, however, with hearts full of joy we got on board the Guernfey, our ranfom being paid to the Moors at the fame time they releafed us out of their hands."

cused publicly of no other crimes than that of trading in the Portuguese dominions, a thing forbidden to any friar, tho' the jesuits certainly carried on an extensive commerce. Upon their being suspended from the *cure of souls,* the father general of the order sent a letter or memorial to Rome. It was written after the new pope's (Rezzonico) accession to the throne, and couched in the following terms, tho' I have shortened the length of the original.

" Most holy father,

" The general of the society of Jesus,
" prostrate at the feet of your holiness,
" humbly represents the extreme grief and
" sorrow that all the order experiences up-
" on account of many rumours scattered
" about the kingdom of Portugal, which
" attribute crimes of the most heinous
" nature to some of them living in the do-
" minions of his most faithful majesty.

" This

" This court having obtained a brief from
" Benedict the Fourteenth of pious memory,
" by which he named reformer and visitor
" with the most ample powers the cardinal Sal-
" dania, in virtue of it the said most eminent
" patriarch has published an edict, wherein
" he declares our whole order universally
" guilty of negociation. Besides this his
" eminence has suspended from preaching
" and confessing not only all the jesuits in-
" habiting the city of Lisbon, but all in
" general throughout these dominions, not-
" withstanding the laws by which bishops
" are deprived of this prohibitive power
" against any whole order of religious per-
" sons without first consulting the holy see.
" And to add to the severity of this prohibi-
" tion, not only notice was given to us of
" the said suspension from preaching and
" confessing, but the edict was ordered to
" be fixed up publicly in all the churches of
" Lisbon. Of all this the father general
" has in his custody authentic testimonies.

" The

"The religious jesuits of Portugal have
"suffered orders like these, so offensive to
"the honor of the whole society, with a
"humility and submission worthy of them.
"They doubt not of the right intention of
"his most faithful majesty, nor of that of
"the most eminent cardinal and other mi-
"nisters under him, yet still they dread left
"these may have been artificially pre-occu-
"pied by calumnious persons, as they can
"never persuade themselves, that any of
"their body are guilty of such henious
"crimes as the world attributes to them,
"especially as they have not been convicted
"of them in any court of justice, nay have
"not even had the liberty of producing
"their defences and allegations.

"And even supposing they were guilty
"of the heinous crimes so unjustly laid to
"their charge, yet still they hope offences
"of so high a nature are not common to all,
"nor to the major part of their order, tho'
"they

" they all behold themselves comprehended
" in one promiscuous punishment. And
" finally, were all the jesuits residing in his
" most faithful majesty's dominions guilty
" from the first to the last, which cannot
" be supposed, yet still our order begs to be
" heard with candour, and more especially
" those who, in all other parts of the world,
" strive with most indefatigable diligence to
" promote, as far as lies in their power, the
" honor of God and the salvation of their
" neighbour.

" Now the discredit and damage, which
" attends such aspersions, are extended to all
" the order, an order which abhors even the
" name of those crimes which are imputed
" to them, and would not willingly do any
" thing that might offend either the ecclesi-
" astical or civil power.

" It is upon this account that the mem-
" bers of it wish with the greater ardor to
" see

" see themselves justified from calumnies of
" which they esteem themselves undeserv-
" ing.

" The superiors of the order have only
" begged that they at least might be privately
" informed of the guilty persons, and of the
" proofs against them, and that they would be
" the first in cutting off all those abuses that
" may have been introduced; but the hum-
" ble supplication and offers of the supe-
" riors were not thought worthy of atten-
" tion.

" Care must be taken lest, instead of a
" profitable reformation, rise be given to
" unprofitable disturbances, which, indeed,
" are much to be feared at present in the
" countries beyond sea. All that cardinal
" Saldania acts of himself, we have not the
" least doubt of his performing in the best and
" most just manner, but we are, with reason,
" afraid, that the persons he may appoint
" to

"to transact affairs abroad should, through ignorance or ill will, imbroil matters still more than they are at present.

"The general, therefore, of the society of Jesus, as well for himself, as in the name of all the order, implores your holiness to attend to this their humble entreaty, and in consequence of it, they supplicate you to use your authority, and to act as your high understanding shall think best, to the end that those who are innocent may be indemnified by a justification of their actions, as also to provide for the just and profitable amendment of those who may be guilty, and, in short, for the credit of the whole order, that they may with the greater honor promote the service of God, and the salvation of souls, serving the holy see with all thankfulness, and imitating the pious zeal of your holiness, for whom the general as well as the order shall pray to the Omnipotent,

" potent, to shower upon your holiness all
" the blessings of heaven for many years to
" come, to the joy and prosperity of the
" universal church."

The answer from Clement the Thirteenth to this memorial was very strong against the jesuits. He says that the late pope had appointed cardinal Saldania as visitor, that what he had done was right, nor was it doubted but he had sufficient reasons for his proceedings; that as for the credit of the order, it was their business not to have lost it by committing actions unworthy of it. That with regard to the decree prohibiting them from preaching and confessing, it appeared to be just, as persons who did not take a proper care of their own souls, seemed very unfitting to have those of the faithful committed to their charge, and of whom, in that case, it might be justly said, *medice cura teipsum.* That their objecting to the persons whom cardinal Saldania might nominate to
transact

tranfact the affairs beyond fea was confiderred as ridiculous, and calling in queftion the propriety of their judges before they knew who thofe judges were to be. As to their defire that the court of Rome fhould interfere in this bufinefs, the pope affured them that it would look very particular if, after his predeceffor had appointed cardinal Saldania to manage the affair, he was to fnatch from that prelate's hands the authority conferred upon him, and that without any fufficient reafon; befides which, it was certain that the court of Portugal would very unwillingly fuffer a caufe begun in their ftates to be transferred to Rome.

It was thefe feverities, which the court of Portugal is faid to have ufed its utmoft underhand endeavours to get fhewn towards the jefuits, together with more open infults which the fame court offered them, that determined their order to blow up the flame of the affaffination of the king, being incited
partly

partly by revenge, and partly by intereſt, as hoping their affairs would go on better under a new reign. I have in this paper told you a little what the jeſuits did before the fatal ſtroke, and in my next I will endeavour to inform you what has been done to them ſince that time, but clouds and darkneſs intercept my path.

The comet ſaid to be foretold ſo many years ago by Sir Iſaac Newton for the year 1758, has at length appeared in theſe climates. The Windſor man of war has brought a French Eaſt Indiaman outward bound, into this port.

LET-

LETTER XXV.

LISBON, APRIL 8, 1759.

AFTER the fatal attempt of the third of September was put into execution, nothing was immediately done to the jesuits; however, about the time of the nobles being taken up, those of that society in Lisbon were confined to their convents; and after the execution of the nobles, a strict order of confinement was issued out against all the jesuits in the king's dominions. The orders are given in a letter from the king himself, which he addresses to one of his magistrates. It is as follows.

" To Pedro Gonsalvez Cordeiro Pereira
" of our council, chancellor of the Casa
" de Supplicaçaon and our friend,
" I the king greeting.

" The

"The pernicious machinations, scanda-
"lous seditions, revolutions, and declared
"wars excited by the religious persons of
"the society of Jesus in these kingdoms
"and their dominions, and which are at
"this time manifest to all Europe, gave us
"just and indispensible motives of com-
"plaining of their proceedings to the holy fa-
"ther Benedict the fourteenth, then president
"of the universal church of God; hoping
"that his wisdom, without proceeding to
"extremities, might be able to repress those
"great disorders. But the Jesuits so far
"from being sensible of our religious cle-
"mency, grew the more insolent, and in-
"stead of submitting humbly to the pun-
"ishments that were inflicted upon them,
"dared with arrogance never before seen or
"heard of, to deny the truth of those
"crimes that were alledged against them.
"Not content with this, they have lately
"published their insolent excuses, and have
"proceeded to other steps yet more infa-
            "mous

"mous and rash, by having pretended to
" alienate our loyal subjects from that love
" and fidelity to their sovereign, by which
" the Portuguese above all other civilized
" nations have heretofore been distinguished;
" perverting to this most horrid end the
" sacred mysteries of our religion, and by
" means of them communicating and spread-
" ing abroad the poisonous contagion of
" their sacrilegious calumnies against us,
" and against our government, till they
" arrived at last to form within our very
" capital the horrid conspiracy, treason and
" parricide, of which they as well as the
" other criminals have been convicted. In
" proof of which adjoining to these pre-
" sents we send you a copy of the original
" trial signed by Sebastian Joseph de Car-
" valho of our council, and secretary of
" state for domestic affairs; and to this trial
" you are to give the same credit as if you
" had been present at the original sentence
" passed the twelfth of this present month

" of January in our court of high treason.
" The public necessity, therefore, obliges
" us to make use of that power which God
" hath put into our hands, to maintain and
" defend our royal person and government,
" as well as the public repose of our faith-
" ful subjects, against the insults and incon-
" ceivable rashness of this perfidious order.
" However, we feel due sorrow in not being
" able to dispense with proceeding to these
" last remedies, in which we shall confine
" ourselves to what the kings our most re-
" ligious predecessors, as well as other
" princes and states in Europe, equally ca-
" tholic and pious, have done in cases of
" treason and rebellion committed by eccle-
" siastical persons even of the highest digni-
" ties, and in cases less flagrant than the
" present.

" We therefore command you (tho' not
" upon account of our own authority, but
" only from the indispensible and natural
" obliga-

"obligation we lie under to confult the
"defence of our own royal perfon and
"government, as well as for the tranquillity
"of our dominions and fubjects, till we can
"recur to the apoftolical fee,) as foon as
"you fhall receive thefe prefents to order a
"general fequefter to be made of all the
"effects, rents and penfions which the
"aforefaid Jefuits may enjoy throughout thefe
"realms; naming what affiftants you think
"requifite for the tranfaction of this affair,
"and forming inventories of the effects
"found in each of the religious houfes;
"making a fchedule of the rents and pen-
"fions certain or uncertain belonging to every
"one of the faid religious houfes; which
"rents and penfions are, as they become
"due, to be locked up in coffers with three
"keys; one of which is to be given to the
"truftees chofen by you, another to the
"corregidors of the Comarcas, or their
"deputies, and a third to the fcriveners of
"the Correiçaon; keeping within the faid

"coffers

" coffers the books of revenues and expences
" which shall occur after the beginning of
" the execution of this order. When you
" shall have put into execution all these
" sequestrations, you shall give in to our
" secretary of state a general specification,
" written in a good and legible character, of
" the annual revenues of all and of each of
" the said religious houses, together with
" the sum total of their respective amounts.

" Now as it is not our intention that, in the
" churches, ministers should be wanting to
" the divine functions, much less that lega-
" cies left for masses and other holy works
" should not be complied with; our will is,
" that out of the beforementioned coffers
" there be taken by your order those sums
" of money that may be wanted for the pre-
" parations of masses, celebrations of divine
" offices, and complying with the wills of
" testators who have left sums of money to
" pious uses. Our pleasure also is, that you
likewise

" likewife take out of the faid coffers the
" money neceffary for the maintenance of
" the Jefuits, all of whom we command to
" retire to their refpective convents and
" houfes; and to each of whom we grant
" for their fubfiftence the fum of one tef-
" toon a day, (about fixpence Englifh,) for
" befides the abounding proofs we have al-
" ready had with regard to the theological,
" moral and political errors, which this
" order has endeavoured to fpread about the
" city with fuch pernicious and deteftable
" effects, we have received certain intelligence
" that they now pretend with more anxious
" diligence to corrupt the provinces with
" the fame falfe and abominable doctrines.
" We order, moreover, that all lay brothers
" and coadjutors fpiritual that may be fcat-
" tered feparately up and down the country
" be likewife apprehended and conveyed
" (all their papers being firft feized) under
" fure cuftody, and by the fhorteft way, to
" their principal convents and houfes in the

" cities

" cities or notable villages that are neareſt
" to where they ſhall be taken up, in which
" places they ſhall be confined with the
" other Jeſuits, and lie under a ſimilar ex-
" preſs prohibition of going out, or of com-
" municating with our ſecular ſubjects.
" We command you alſo to take care that
" military guards be always in their ſight,
" who ſhall oblige them exactly to perform
" this ſecluſion, until we order the contrary.
" And for the execution of theſe our orders,
" we command that you be aſſiſted by the
" military power, which you may require
" at pleaſure, ordering the generals and per-
" ſons charged with the command of our
" armies, as well in the reſpective provinces
" as at this court, to aid and aſſiſt you with-
" out any limitation, as often as you ſhall
" require it in our royal name, with liberty
" to command any number of troops to
" march, which you or the magiſtrates ap-
" pointed by you ſhall think neceſſary, as
" well to the places where the ſequeſters
" are

"are to be made, as to the convents and houses where the jesuits are to be confined; to the end that those guards may secure the aforesaid houses, and inspect the strict seclusion that the Jesuits are to observe in them, as is done in this capital. We judge it unnecessary to use any urgent expressions to excite your diligence in this weighty affair, as we are conscious of the great zeal, fidelity and rectitude which you have always manifested in our royal service.

"Given at our palace this 19th day of January, 1759.

"I the King."

I shall set out to night at ten o'clock for Seville, but shall only cross the river Tagus, to be ready in the morning for proceeding upon my journey.

LETTER XXVI.

BEJA, APRIL 12, 1759.

ALL that we know further about the jefuits than what I have mentioned, is, that Cordeira Pereira punctually executed the orders received from the king, which I fent you in my laft. All the jefuits are confined to their refpective convents, and a ftrict guard placed over them. Some of the principals, as, indeed, I faid before, are in prifon, of whofe deftiny we are entirely ignorant. In the mean time their caufe is examining in the court of Rome, and I imagine after things are fettled there, the determination will be publifhed concerning the whole body, which moft people think will be totally exterminated out of Portugal, and the order of the

pious

pious schools introduced in their stead. This, tho' little, is all we know, and I believe time alone will discover thoroughly the proceedings of this court. They would willingly, I think, bring some jesuits to public execution, but they seem afraid of openly attacking an order so formidable in the Roman catholic religion, as the minds of the vulgar are strongly prepossessed in favor of every thing that has the outward appearance of sanctity.

I will now give you some description of my journey from Lisbon to this place, where I have been very kindly received into the house of a gentleman to whom I brought a letter. As this is the holy week, which is not proper for travelling, especially in Roman catholic countries, I shall stay here from this present Thursday till Monday next, when I shall continue my route towards Seville. I left Lisbon upon the 8th in the evening (having, as I said in my former letter, to cross the river Tagus) that I might be ready to

ascend

ascend my chaise early in the morning, and continue my journey. The place I was to lay at is called Aldea-galega, about twelve English miles from Lisbon. As the moon shone bright my little voyage was rendered very agreeable by her rays. I was pulled along with eight oars, and being assisted by the tide glided swiftly through the water. The city of Lisbon looks extremely pleasant from the Tagus, as the houses are situated upon little hills, and rise gradually one above another, which forms a most delightful view. The brightness of the moon rendered the town more conspicuous, yet her beams were not strong enough to display the horrors of it, and make the ruins visible, which in the day time look melancholy from the spot in which we then were. The river in this place is between two or three leagues over. Upon our landing we found the inn full of travellers, which put us to more distress for accommodations than we should otherwise have suffered even in this inhospitable

table country. At about three o'clock in the morning the poſtilion hurried me up, tho' it was paſt four before we ſet out. Upon my coming into the open air the firſt thing that ſtruck my eye-ſight was the comet, who ſeemed to ſcowl inauſpiciouſly upon my journey. I ſuppoſe he muſt now be viſible to you inhabitants of Great Britain. Whether it be the ſame predicted by Sir Iſaac Newton, its courſe alone muſt determine. This comet appears to us nearly in the eaſt, with its tail pointing weſtward. Our mules had not drawled us on far, before that beautiful ruddineſs which is the harbinger of the riſing ſun appeared, and ſhortly after the ſun himſelf emerged above the horizon and gilt with his rays that vaſt plain we were then travelling over. The country was as ugly as ever eye beheld. Flat to the laſt degree, except, indeed, ſome diſtant mountains which lay near Liſbon. The ſoil, a deep white ſand, which permitted nothing to grow, but thoſe ſorts of ſhrubs which flouriſh upon the moſt

barren

barren heaths in thefe countries. The reflection from it gave redoubled power to the fun, which being now very high, made us fenfible of its force, tho' the heat was tempered from time to time by an agreeable cloud, which, however, are not very frequent in thefe fine climates. About ten o'clock we arrived at our baiting place, which was the firſt houfe we had feen fince we left Aldea-galega. Our inn had, indeed, three or four other buildings to keep it company, but every thing elfe was nearly as wild and defert as ever. As foon as my chaife ſtopt I difmounted. In England and other countries the landlord and landlady come out and make their compliments to the ſtrangers, in Spain and Portugal things feem quite different, for you muſt go and pay your refpects to them. To comply then with the cuſtom of the country, I went into the kitchen, and pulled off my hat in great form to a lady who was fitting by the fire fide, tho' it was burning hot, and whofe looks told me ſhe was the miſtrefs of

the

the houfe. She got up and returned me a bowing courtefy with all the folemnity imaginable. In fhort, many compliments paffed on both fides, in which I endeavoured to change my Spanifh into broken Portuguefe. The refpect I fhewed got me a little fifh for dinner, but the appearance of it, and of the little ugly black woman who brought it in, gave me no defire of tafting it, and I fhould have made a more meagre dinner than any of the Roman catholics, if it had not been for our own provifions, upon which I accomplifhed a hearty meal. As there was a little pine grove nearly oppofite to the inn, I entertained myfelf after dinner with walking in it, and enjoying the few trees of which it was compofed, as the whole morning I had hardly feen a bufh. Upon my return I found the inn crouded with the travellers who lay at Aldeagalega the evening before. They were Italians, and I thought they were to keep to the left hand to go to Madrid, but they had made a little round for the fake of

feeing

seeing Evora the capital of Alentejo, the province in which I am at present. Our conversation turned with justice upon the very bad travelling through Spain and Portugal, till the appearance of my chaise interrupted it. We never thought of meeting again, as I was to go to Silveres that night, and they only to Ventas Novas two leagues short of it, and accordingly we took leave of each other, with reciprocal wishes of a good journey. I proceeded in the afternoon through a country not much better than what we had experienced in the morning, however we did meet with two or three houses, at one of which I bought a large cargo of oranges, which in the meanest cottages are to be found in the greatest perfection. Upon our coming to Silveres we met with nearly the same treatment as in the former inn, with a supper nearly as bad, which, however, I had not finished, when I heard two chaises stop at the door, and upon looking out of the window, I saw my new acquaintances the Italians

Italians getting out of them. They had come on farther than they intended, and I spent a very merry evening with them, till midnight informed us that it was time for travellers to retire to rest.

LETTER XXVII.

LA PUEBLA, APRIL 19, 1759.

I AM now at the firſt little town in the Spaniſh dominions, and a poor little place it is; but to bring you here in due order I muſt continue my narration.

The Sun had no ſooner riſen upon us at Silveres than I was ſeparated from my new companions, and purſued my route towards Beja. They ſtruck off to the left for Badajos. We had ſtill, however, another chaiſe in company, in which was a Portugueſe gentleman, who was carrying his daughter to take the veil at Viana; but they were ſo very reſerved, it was impoſſible to have much communication with them. Indeed, one of the characteriſtics of the Portugueſe

ſeems

seems to be an aversion, or I may say hatred, to foreigners. We dined at a little village called St. Jago, from whence we were conducted thro' a very ugly country to Viana, the place where I lay that night. Tho' the country from Lisbon to Viana had resembled what I wrote to you of near Aldeagalega, yet just by that town it was prettily interspersed with groves of olive trees, situated upon little rising hills. Our inn and accommodations we still thought very bad, but nothing to be compared with what I have since experienced in Spain. Here you find nothing in the inns, if, indeed, there are any, but a very dirty room, and what you eat or drink must be brought with you, or you are obliged to run about the place and buy it yourself. The intended nun and her father left us at Viana, nor will I detain you longer in a town where there is nothing to divert you; and was hardly any thing for me to eat.

The reason of so great a want of provisions, was our having been overturned just in entering Viana, which had blended no small quantity of sandy dirt with our stock. Some priests, however, according to the hospitality of the country, gave us part of their provisions, which with what I got at the inn made up a poor supper. The next day we dined at Cuba, a little village not above twelve miles from Beja. Every thing was very good here, as they had been previously informed of my coming by my Beja friends. A comfortable nap after dinner, according to the fashion of southern countries, being finished, we set out, and arrived at Beja above an hour before sun-set. It is situated upon a hill which continues gently rising for a great many miles every way round it. This gives a very extensive prospect from every part over a fruitful corn country, the only one of that kind of any extent, I believe, in the kingdom; and which is almost as destitute of trees as our downs, except, indeed,

deed, a few olive groves on that side towards Seville. I met with many civilities from the inhabitants of this town, or city, for so you must call it to please them. The first day I passed there my landlord's mother would not appear at table, on account of the tyrannical custom in Portugal, which renders it indecent for a lady to be visible when there are strangers in the house. However, by strong intercession, she came down the day after, without any of those charms which might make her appearance of consequence.

As an exact journal of what I did at Beja must be tiresome, I will only tell you that I had there an opportunity of seeing much more of the Portuguese than all the time I remained at Lisbon. One evening I spent very agreeably at a gentleman's country house about three or four miles from the place, and just in that part where the olive trees are situated. An alcove placed under some orange trees, and by the side of a little pond

pond, gave us an opportunity of enjoying the fresh breezes that blew and tempered the heat of the Sun, which we have already experienced much greater than at any time in England. A profusion of sweatmeats and other good things were set before us, to which we added oranges and sweet lemons that we gathered ourselves from the impending branches. As we were walking afterwards round the garden, a large serpent thwarted our way. I believe he was a yard and a half in length. I had never seen one so big, and, indeed, he was a very fine sight. When he found we intended to kill him, he put himself in a posture of defence. He drew his tail and hindermost parts in a circle under him, and raising his head and chest a foot above the ground, darted out his tongue, and seemed to spit venom at us. But stones soon dispatched him, and extended him at his length upon the ground,

As

As it was the holy week, some part of the little time I was at Beja was occupied in seeing Roman catholic functions and ceremonies. They are much more superstitious in those things here than in Italy, and add cruelty to superstition, in permitting the penitents to flog, and torment themselves in other ways, about the streets. The farther you get from Rome, the more such kind of penances are intermixed with religion; and learning seems to banish them entirely from her empire.

As to the Portuguese, they are still fifty years behind other nations. The great cloak thrown over the left shoulder hides every thing. And yet these very people, who owe the comforts of life to foreigners, as their European and Indian dominions produce little more than wine, oil, oranges and gold, begrudge the money paid to other nations for their corn, cloaths, and other more necessary commodities.

LETTER XXVIII.

SEVILLE, APRIL 23, 1759.

After a very fatiguing journey I am at length arrived at this city. But to bring you hither in due order I will continue my narration, the thread of which I shall take up from my leaving Beja, as nothing farther occurred worth mentioning during my stay there.

The postilion had no sooner conducted me out of town, than we beheld the road we were to travel open for many miles before us, for, as I told you in my last, Beja stands upon an eminence. We soon got into a very pretty country intersperfed with olive trees, the same I have already spoken to you about, and the only one of the kind all round Beja,

but

but I foon had a different occupation for my thoughts than confidering the beauties of nature. Through the negligence of our poftilion, for the road was not extremely bad, our chaife wheel gathering upon a right hand bank, fent us and our baggage into a ditch upon the left. I crawled out of the miferable vehicle as well as I could, but the difficulty confifted in getting that upright again. Juft at this time a country man fortunately paffed within a few yards of us, but, to give you an idea of the Portuguefe character, he never offered to ftop or give us the leaft affiftance.

Animated, however, at laft by the offer of fome money, he lent an aukward hand, and after much trouble, (being forced to untie the trunk and all the reft of the baggage,) the chaife ftood once more upon its two wheels, and we continued our journey. The roads were now very bad indeed, or I might perhaps with truth fay, there was no road at all

all till we arrived at the Guadiana. The Guadiana is a river which in a great many parts divides the Portuguefe territory from that of Spain, but not juft in that place I was to pafs it, where there is above a days journey further in the kingdom of Portugal, till you come to a little river called Chanfas, which indeed is a kind of arm of the Guadiana, and feparates the two dominions by its ftream. As there was no road down to the Guadiana but over plowed grounds, you can hardly imagine there was any bridge to pafs it. Inftead of a bridge there ftood a fine antique ferry boat, with two men in it, who appeared of equal antiquity with the bark, and who, upon feeing us come down to the river, conveyed their veffel to our fide. Here we were forced again to untie all our baggage and take off the mules, in fhort, lofe much time before we could get into the boat, and at leaft as much in getting out of it again.

As

As the way from Beja to the Guadiana had been nearly a constant descent, from the Guadiana to Serpa, the place where I was to dine, was almost all up hill, and some part very steep. The winter torrents had so spoiled the road, which they pretended to have once been here, that the chaise was obliged to quarter between clefts almost big enough to swallow half of it. You may imagine I did not keep my seat during all these precipices, especially after having so lately had the specimen of an overthrow. I walked up the steepest part on foot, and as we had set out late in the morning, and had lost much time in our overturn and passing the river, it was now near two o'clock, and the sun struck upon us with inexpressible heat. It was near four o'clock before we got to the inn at Serpa, so that it was impossible to continue our journey after dinner, especially as we wanted to provide ourselves with a guide, for the chaise-man knew nothing of the way, nor could we get any other at Beja.

Indeed,

Indeed, I did very wrong ever to come to Beja in my route from Lisbon to Seville; but I was over-persuaded by my friends there, who told me it was the shortest and best way. It certainly is the shortest; but I do not doubt if I had gone by Badajos I should have arrived much sooner and more easily at Seville. But these reflections were now too late, so that I applied my thoughts to finding out a good guide, and for that end determined to apply to a gentleman for whom I had a letter. But as I felt myself fatigued, I deferred my visit till I had eaten a mouthful, and afterwards, instead of making it, laid myself down upon a couple of ordinary mattrasses extended upon the floor, where I slept till sun-set.

LETTER XXIX.

SEVILLE, APRIL 29, 1759.

AFTER having repofed myfelf at Serpa, my landlord, who was a Spaniard, conducted me to the perfon I was recommended to, who promifed to procure me a guide that knew every inch of the way over the mountains. Upon my return I found two fentries with halberts in their hands planted at the ftreet door of my inn. The landlady came running out and informed me, that the governor of Serpa was come to make me a vifit. I fincerely believe, however, that under this mafk of civility he wanted to be informed who I was that was leaving the kingdom; and indeed the confufed ftate of Portugal might well juftify orders of that nature from the government. Upon my coming into the

room

room he addressed me with a profusion of compliments. As we had no chairs, I advanced a joint stool for his excellency to sit upon, and we began a conversation in which I laboured hard to make myself intelligible. After staying about half an hour he arose, and telling me he had importuned me with that visit only to know if it was in his power to do me any service, he marched off with his military attendants. * * * * * *
* * * * * * * * * * * *

LETTER XXX.

SEVILLE, MAY 3, 1759.

I Spent my evening at Serpa with the gentleman to whom I was recommended. His family confisted of a wife and two pretty girls between eighteen and twenty. Upon my coming in I found the old lady feated in a low chair, and her two daughters upon two round mats placed upon the ground, where they were fitting like taylors. It is faid, the common people of Portugal have but newly introduced the cuftom of chairs, which the great refort of foreigners to Lifbon has given them an idea of. It is very odd fometimes upon entering into country houfes to fee the good ladies all fitting upon the floor like fo many Turks; and, indeed, I believe thefe are fome remains of

Moorifh

Moorish customs, as those infidels were a long time in possession of Portugal and of Spain likewise; especially in the part where I am at present. It is for this reason, that the Spanish and Portuguese languages abound with Moorish words, and I dare say, the great number of guttural syllables in the former were derived from that origin. But not to detain you any longer in Serpa, I will pass over my bad fare that evening, and place you with me in the chaise the morning after, into which I mounted before it was light. In going out of the town I stopt at my friend's door, who gave me a letter to an acquaintance of his that lived at Corte de Pinto, where I was to lay that night. After many compliments and many embraces, which the Portuguese always burden you with, popping their head from the left to the right shoulder, I at last got rid of my very good, but very ceremonious friend, and the chaise once more rolled on. We were five persons in all, I and my servant

servant made two, the postilion three, the fourth was our guide on foot, and my landlord of the day before made the fifth; who being to go to a place some miles in Spain, chose to walk it with the guide, rather than at some other time travel thro' all that barren country alone.

I forgot to tell you that our postilion had taken with him from Beja the longest largest broadest broad sword that ever was beheld, much too heavy for himself to carry; and which was deposited in a sort of place made on purpose to suspend it, upon the left front of the saddle of the mule he rode. Here it hung like a scarecrow, for it was altogether as rusty as large, and the point had mouldered its way through the bottom of the scabbard. But now, with the addition of our two men on foot, we had acquired two other sabres of the same kind, which being likewise too heavy to carry, one was adjusted upon the mule that bore the shafts, and the other fixed behind the chaise upon my trunk. These, besides the arms I had, consisting of four pistols and two swords, formed our military furniture. You may wonder to hear me talk of pistols, having told you, I think, in my letters about the affairs of Lisbon, that all fire arms had been taken away from the Portuguese, and consequently, prohibited to be carried openly. Let it suffice for me to say, that at the same time I got my passport from the secretary of state for foreign affairs Don Lewis da Cunia, I got a licence for carrying pistols included.

Equipped and accompanied in this manner, I went on thro' a most miserably desert country indeed, where no mortal seemed to have set his foot. It was hilly, tho' the hills were not very high, but then so barren, that it hardly afforded a tree; however, there was plenty of undergrowth, and many shrubs, some of which smelt extremely aromatical, inatical, for lavender, thyme, and balm of gilead, if I miftake not, and fome other plants of this nature grow wild in thefe countries. Road there was none, for as very few chaifes pafs the way I came from Lifbon to Seville, every paffenger makes a track of his own. Having travelled on in this manner for not a few miles, fometimes getting out of the chaife for bad precipices, and at others being able to fit in it, we at laft arrived to the place where we were to dine. You may think it was an inn, but you would be miftaken. It was a little knowl of trees ftanding upon a rifing ground. Here we alighted from our chaife, pulled out our provifions, and fat ourfelves down upon the grafs. In the mean time, the poftilion took off the mules, and fupported the two fhafts of the carriage upon the low branch of a tree. After he had done this, he tied his mules one on one fide of the chaife, and the other on the other; and made a manger of the place where you fet your feet, which you will find will anfwer that purpofe very well, if you reprefent to your idea an Englifh open poft chaife with two wheels, or a one horfe chair. After the two beafts were adjufted we fat down in a ring, and began making our rural meal in all peace and quietnefs.

LETTER XXXI.

SEVILLE, MAY 6, 1759.

AFTER we had finished our romantic dinner under the knowl of trees mentioned in my last, the postilion hung pieces of paper upon some of the branches, in token of his having made a repast there, as well as to direct him and the guide in their way back, for it is now time to inform you that our new guide knew nothing of the road. While the mules were putting too I was inclined to take a walk, but was desired not to separate myself from the rest for fear of wolves or other accidents, with what foundation I cannot say.

Every thing being at length in order for our departure, we proceeded on our journey to Corte de Pinto, the moſt miſerable village I ever beheld, ſituated in the midſt of that wild country. This was the place where we were to paſs the night, to an inhabitant of which I had brought a letter from Serpa. The perſon not being at home, but at a farm a mile or two off, I was obliged to diſpatch a meſſenger to him, and in the mean time ſat down upon a ſtone bench at the door of the hut which belonged to my unknown friend, and which, he not being there, was locked up. Tho' I call it a hut, it was one of the beſt edifices in the place. The poſtilion during this interval took off his mules, and turned them grazing upon a ſort of green before the door, a common cuſtom in theſe countries, where their cattle very often live at the expence of the public. The whole pariſh, men, women, and children, ſoon gathered all about us, and ſeemed to ſtare as if we had fallen from the ſtars. A trifle of charity I gave to a little girl who had

got

got a diftaff faftened into her girdle, according to the fafhion of thefe countries, and was fpinning away very diligently, and which I told her was for her induftry, caufed many others to appear in a fhort time equipped in like manner, and form a fpinning party round about me. It was now near fun-fet, and I was anxious about not feeing my friend, but at laft he appeared ftriding over the green with the perfon I had fent for him. Compliments having paffed, which he returned in an honeft plain country manner, he opened his hut, and my goods were carried into it. He then with authority, for he feemed to command all the village, ordered a country man to kill a kid, and get it dreffed for fupper. In the mean time we entered into converfation, which I was obliged to maintain as well as I could. He faid it was above four years fince a chaife had paffed that way, and that the road next day would be much worfe than what I had paffed. For my farther confolation the guide

came

came and confessed his ignorance of the way, excusing himself, however, upon his having just heard that the winter torrents had spoiled the road he used to go, and that none but a country man born upon the spot would be able to conduct us through the very bye and round about course we must take. I was forced to acquiesce, and a second guide was hired, which was the less disagreeable to me, as in those terrible roads where every moment you may expect overturns, an assistant or two on foot is very useful, not to mention their being a kind of defence to those who pass through such very desert places. Having settled these preliminaries, and our kid being ready, we sat down to our patriarchal supper, which, notwithstanding the animal's being fresh killed, was far from the worst I had made, and was succeeded by a good hard but clean country bed. My host in the morning would not accept of any thing for the trouble and expence to which I had put him. The same assemblage of country

try people flocked about my chaife as the evening before, however, at laſt on we moved, and left the ruſtic multitude gazing behind us.

LETTER XXXII.

SEVILLE, MAY 10, 1759.

FROM Corte de Pinto to the Spanish territory is not above three miles, and those not the longest. The two kingdoms are separated in this place by a little river, as I mentioned before, called Chanfas. Besides this boundary of water there is a chain of hills, tho' not very high, called the Sierra Morena, which also divide Spain from Portugal for some way, and afterwards run on into Spain. You will find in Don Quixote this hilly, barren country, renowned for many of his adventures, and, indeed, it seems calculated for the mansion of desperate knights-errant. Our company was the same as before, except the addition of our new guide,

guide, who was leading us through briars and brambles, where there was not the least sign of any person's having passed before. However we at last arrived at the river Chansas, which tho' it had not rained for some time, was higher than it ought to be. There had been a dispute the evening before, whether we could go over or no, which had been determined in the affirmative, and so indeed we did, but not without some difficulty.

We had no sooner set our feet upon Spanish ground than all snuff boxes were opened and our Portuguese and foreign snuff given to the winds. They are so very strict here that a pinch is enough to send a common person to the galleys and forfeit all his goods. I do not see the policy of this government in so entirely excluding all foreign snuff from the kingdom. They are, without doubt, in the right to give all the advantages they can to their own manufactures. But

might

might not a high tax be of equal advantage to their adminiftration, as that upon French wines to ours? To prove how ftrict the Spaniards are with regard to this commodity, I will juft mention a cafe that happened lately. Two Irifh lads, of which nation there are a great many of the Roman catholics, who fend their children to be educated here, coming from Cadiz to Seville, one of them thoughtlefsly happened in an inn to pull out a fnuff box, in which were two or three pinches of rappee. A foldier who faw it took the fnuff box from him, with the lofs of which they contented themfelves, thinking all was over. But they were afterwards taken up at Seville and thrown in prifon, where they ftaid till intereft and money at length delivered them from durance. What renders thefe countries more rigorous is their farming out all thefe forts of things. The government receives fo many thoufands a year from fuch a perfon, who is generally the beft bidder, to whom they grant the licence of

being

being sole manufacturer of some commodity, as for example of snuff, spirituous liquors, silks, cloths, &c. These tenants must be defended by government, or else none would find it worth while to pay such large annual sums, to reimburse which with interest they often oppress the subject. This also may be the reason why other commodities of the same kind highly taxed, are not admitted into the kingdom, as it would create much confusion to the *financiers*.

But to return to our caravan that was now moving gently along upon the confines of Spain, which as yet entirely resembled what I had just passed of Portugal in barrenness and the nature of the country. After we had gone on for about a couple of hours the postilion stopt under some trees, and told us it was breakfast time. Accordingly we pulled out our provisions, and were enjoying them, when a Spaniard joined us.

He

He was a country man and had a dog and gun to kill some game in those dreary wastes. The different look of him from the Portuguese, the different dress and different language struck me, how in the space of a mile or two there could be such a change in the inhabitants. I have heard people say that the Portuguese and Spaniards are very much alike in their customs and every thing. I cannot say I have found them so. It is true in their appearance they are both black, but then there is a majesty generally in the look of a Spaniard which the Portuguese seem greatly to want. The Spanish language too is much more sonorous than the Portuguese, nor do the great quantity of gutturals in it displease me. Besides, I think, I like the Spanish dress better than the Portuguese. It consists, indeed, of a cloak thrown a second time over the left shoulder, but of a different make, colour and air from that of the Portuguese. This, with a sort of net over their hair,

hair, and a great flapped hat, compleats the common dress of an inhabitant of Andalusia, the province in which Seville is situated. Not but that Spaniards put on coats sometimes, however, it is rare at this distance from Madrid, except among the military gentlemen. Some of them are very curious when they dress out. Being used to their cloak, they find themselves unhappy without it. Their cloaths set upon them in a very aukward manner, their waistcoat gets up to their chin, and their sword seems to run through their haunches. In Cadiz, however, the flapped hat is forbidden to be used, as it is a very populous town, and the government has a mind to see the inhabitants' faces as they walk along the streets. For really this same dark coloured cloak with a flapped hat, is as total a disguise to the men as the veils are to the women.

I have

I have made so long a digression that I seem almost to have forgotten my journey, but I will bring you back to it in my next paper.

LETTER XXXIII.

SEVILLE, MAY 14, 1759.

OUR breakfaſt with the hunting Spaniard and my dependents being finiſhed, we continued our journey. I had this morning another overturn, but received no hurt. About a mile before we ſtopped to dine, we came to a place ſimilar to which, I believe, was never yet paſſed by wheels. Beſides briers and brambles, it was ſo very uneven and ſo ſteep a deſcent, that we were forced to tie a rope round the chaiſe, and hold it up with all our force. At laſt we got to the bottom, and croſſed a little river, the name of which I do not remember. As ſoon as we were arrived on the other ſide, we adjuſted ourſelves under ſome trees, and dined as the day before, only with this advantage, that we had water just by us for ourselves and the mules to drink; but the day before we had been obliged to travel some miles after our meal, before we could get any. Wine, indeed, we had in plenty, but that alone is a bad allayer of thirst; and it had taken so strong a taste of the goat-skin bottle it was contained in, that to me it was extremely disagreeable; tho' some people in England, not knowing whence it proceeds, say they like the taste of the *Boracha* or skin vessel. We were hardly set down upon the grass when a shepherd joined us, whom we made our guest, as we had done with the man in the morning, and which is, indeed, always the custom of these parts of Spain; where every person will eat your provision without any ceremony, and give you theirs without any reluctance.

Nothing very remarkable happened to us. In the evening we got quietly to the little village where we were to lay that night. The name

name of it is La Puebla. Upon our arrival at the inn, I was obliged to conform to the Spanish custom of sending all about the place to buy every little thing we wanted. All the necessaries of life are very dear in Spain, which must be the case of a country that abounds in gold, and nothing else. The good effects of industry and commerce cannot be stronger proved than by considering the great quantity of gold and silver the Spaniards have in the West Indies; and yet, at home, in many cases they want common conveniences. Gold alone can never make a nation plentiful, on the contrary, that very gold must go to other kingdoms to buy what the indolence of the inhabitants denies them in their native country. We ought, however, by no means to attempt to open their eyes. Their blindness is of too much service to England, not to wish them to continue in it. When you consider the two countries, what I have said will appear stronger. The climate of Spain would pro-

duce, they say, every sort of commodity necessary for the wants or luxury of life, that of England is too cold for many; and yet, the balance of commerce, notwithstanding long wars, during which the French introduced their manufactures, is infinitely in our favor; and I dare say they receive twice as many goods from us as we from them. * * * * * * * * * *
* * * * * * * * * * * *

LETTER XXXIV.

SEVILLE, MAY 17, 1759.

NOT to keep you continually in inns, I will omit what trivial occurences happened to me in La Puebla, where the cuftom-houfe people tumbled about all my things, miftaking tooth powder for fnuff; and will feat you with me in the chaife upon our journey the next morning. I will, however, tell you, that before we could get away, the poftilion was obliged to give fecurity for returning the fame road he came with his chaife and mules. I do not know the reafon of this law, which feems calculated for the inconvenience of coachmen, without any immediate benefit to the ftate; and, indeed, the poor poftilion found a gentleman at Seville, who would have taken his chaife quite to Lisbon by Badajos, but not the way I came. He was certainly in the right, as it was only a road for breaking necks.

After we had travelled on for about five or six hours from this first dirty village in Spain, we came to our baiting place, which was in the open fields as before, but with this disadvantage, that we had not a single tree to shade us. The sun struck upon our heads with unremitting fury, and when we got into our chaise, it felt like an oven. In our progress we met a patrole of guards, who roam in parties about these wilds, to hinder any counterband trade between Spain and Portugal, which however, is every day carried on by the Spaniards. I have heard them reckoned the boldest smugglers of any nation; and they say, that during our last war with Spain, they kept up a continual underhand trade with Gibraltar, bringing provisions and other commodities to the garrison; for which some of them were hanged at Cadiz. The patrole of guards at firſt paſſed us, but ſoon after faced about, and ordered us to halt. They were ten in number, five of which with great pomp ranged themſelves on one ſide of the chaiſe, and five on the other. The head or captain then aſked us with a magiſterial voice, if we had got any counterband goods, but upon ſhewing the credentials given us at the cuſtomhouſe of La Puebla, they ſuffered us to proceed. A little before ſun-ſet we arrived at the ſmall town which was to harbour us that night. Its name, if I miſtake not, is Sibiro. We had much trouble from a bridge ſituated at the entrance of it. It ſeemed good at the beginning, but when we came towards the other ſide, for it was very long, one of the arches was broken down. As there was no turning about, we were forced to back the mules all the way. We at laſt, however, croſſed the river, and got to the inn, which was ſo very bad, that rather than lay upon the mattraſs they gave me, or upon the beſt ſtraw they had, I choſe to ſpend the night upon my trunk, with a chair to ſupport my head. I got away as ſoon as poſſible from this dreadful manſion, in which, however, I had the advantage of joining company with ſome honeſt farmers who were going to Seville. We dined under ſome ſycamores that grew near a depopulated village, with old Mooriſh walls. Nor were our accommodations better in the evening than heretofore; but I have already given you too many deſcriptions of bad inns,

LETTER XXXV.

SEVILLE, MAY 21, 1759.

I AM now come to the laſt day of our tedious journey from Beja to Seville, and which, indeed, was as laborious as any; for we had not got many miles before we found the road too narrow for the chaiſe to proceed, and were forced to lift it over many banks. It was alſo twice overturned this morning, but I had the good fortune not to be in it. Beſides all this, we were once ſtuck in a ſlough, out of which, I believe, we ſhould never have been able to get, if we had not been aſſiſted by ſome countrymen's mules. However, we at length came into a greater road, and arrived without any farther accident to St. Lucar, of which name there is a port not far from Cadiz, at the mouth of the

river

river Quadalquivir; but the place where I dined was only a large village of the same denomination. Upon our drawing so near Seville, our fare was much mended, and we found, at least, a possibility of purchasing part of what we wanted. As we had all an inclination of getting to our journey's end as soon as we could, we set out in the face of the burning sun; and after having gone about ten miles, the famous city of Seville stood open to our view. It lies in a valley surrounded by little hills at some miles distance, and towards the south-east the horizon is terminated by very high mountains, which separate this part of Andalusia from Granada. But hereafter I may tell you more of Seville, and shall now only add, that we all entered it in good health, tho' much fatigued. * * * * * * * *
* * * * * * * * * * * *

LETTER XXXVI.

SEVILLE, MAY 24, 1759.

SEVILLE, the ancient Hispalis, is the capital of Andalusia, which, indeed, you know as well as myself. The Spaniards reckon it one of the finest cities in the world, and tell you, that who has not seen *Sevilla,* has not seen *Meravilla,* or a wonder. It certainly is a very handsome town, tho' far from equal to their idea. However, its ancient Moorish walls, which have been lately repaired and painted, make as romantic an appearance as any thing I ever saw. There are few English in this city, but a great many Irish Roman catholic merchants, some of whom are very rich. The true born Spaniard has generally too high a notion of himself to apply to commerce, and much less

less to the menial offices of life, which are mostly performed by French or Italians. During this war, indeed, some of their ships have found their way to London.

Since my residence at Seville, I have always gone into the country for two or three days at the latter end of the week. The place I go to is called La Puebla, not the dirty town I passed thro' in coming to Seville, as you may imagine from its distance, but another more clean little village of the same name upon the banks of the Guadalquivir. (the ancient Betis). I here enjoy a little fresh air and country exercise, in which the vice-consul generally bears me company. You may wonder, perhaps, how there comes to be a vice-consul at so little a village, but I must inform you, that very few ships bound for Seville, come higher up the Quadalquivir than La Puebla, upon account of the danger of the navigation. In many places there are banks of sand, and I never

saw

saw a river wind more in all my life; besides which there is a law that falls very hard upon masters of ships, and this is, that supposing their vessel has the misfortune to run on ground, they are immediately put into prison, till, at their own expence, they have either got her off again, or broke her up, and carried her away by pieces, in order that the channel should not remain incumbered. Now in time of war there are, indeed, fewer ships; but I have heard, that during peace here are sometimes no less than twenty English vessels come in a year to load fruit for London. Many are at present forced to make use of other stratagems, and get what they can under Spanish colours; with other contrivances of the same nature, too common to those who seek only their private emolument.

LETTER XXXVII.

SEVILLE, MAY 29, 1759.

As I am now working hard in perfecting myself in the Spanish language, I must, consequently, read a good many Spanish books, and I have now before me one which has entertained me exceedingly. It is Feyjoo, a modern Spanish author, who writes with much sense and elegance in this very noble language, which I esteem the finest at present spoken in Europe. As for some particular sentiments now and then upon religion, the Spaniards are so bigotted to their own, that these must be expected. Tho' perhaps, if there were no inquisition in Spain, they would not be quite so virulent, as they now may think it more easy to get a licence for the printing of works,

if

if they speak againſt proteſtants. I need not acquaint you that they muſt have a number of licenſes before they can print any of their productions. One from the inquiſition, that there may be nothing againſt the church; one from the civil magiſtrate, that there may be nothing againſt the ſtate; and others from other people, as for monks from their particular order, and ſo on. Theſe reſtraints check the genius of the Spaniards, for naturally they have to be ſure very great talents. But to return to my reading Feyjoo, who is ſtill alive, and is a Benedictine Friar. He calls his works a confutation of all common errors. Moſt of them, indeed, that he takes in hand are ſo common, that any perſon of the leaſt education has already got rid of them; however, his ſtyle is very agreeable, and he now and then runs off into entertaining digreſſions. Notwithſtanding he includes in his work the confutation of ſuch puerile opinions as thoſe of ghoſts, witches and

appari-

apparitions, he rises sometimes to the most learned subjects, and treats of different points of mathematical and philosophical knowledge. The subject of what I have been just now reading is, whether any nation is superior to others in genius. After having weighed separately all nations in the four divisions of the world, he says he thinks not, and that there is no real difference in their natural capacities, but that the being more or less barbarous, is owing to their better or worse education; however, if, says he, there be any (I found these words with pleasure at the end of his essay,) I should give the preference to the English nation. I will translate you his own words at length, as deserving to be read by every British subject.

" If, however, I were to give a prefer-
" ence to any of the European nations above
" the rest in subtlety of genius, I should side
" with Heideger, a German author, who
" gives

" gives that advantage to the Englith.
" Great Britain undoubtedly, fince learning
" has been introduced into that ifland, has
" produced a great number of authors of
" the firſt claſs. It would be too tedious
" for me, were I only to mention thoſe,
" which ſhe has given to the order of Bene-
" dictine and Francifcan monks. I will
" mention, however, three in each of thefe
" two focieties, who ſhine like ſtars of fu-
" perior magnitude. The firſt, viz. the
" Benedictine order enjoyed the venerable
" Bede, the renowned Alcuin, and the fa-
" mous Suiffet. The fecond boaſts of
" Alexander of Hales, the fubtle Scotus,
" and his pupil William Ockham. Car-
" dano makes the following reflexion upon
" theſe two laſt geniuſes, whom he puts in
" the rank of the moſt refined in the world,
" and with regard to whom he remarks,
" Barbaros * ingenio nobis haud efſe infe-
riores,

* " That even the barbarians are not inferior to us in
" talents, fince Britain, tho' divided from the whole
" and

" riores, quandoquidem fub brumæ cœlo
" divifa toto orbe Britannia duos tam clari
" ingenii viros emiferit."

" Nor muſt I omit mentioning, that
" when other nations in Europe hardly
" knew what mathematics were, theſe two
" orders had very celebrated Engliſh mathe-
" maticians in them. Roger Bacon was
" famous in that of the Dominicans. He
" performed fo many wonderful things as
" to be fufpected of magic. Some authors
" fay he went to Rome to clear himſelf
" from that afperfion. The common peo-
" ple invented the fame ſtory with regard
" to him, as they tell of Albert the great,
" that he had conſtructed a brazen head
" which anfwered him any queſtions.
" Oliver * of Malmſbury was no lefs fa-

" world, and placed under a hemiſphere of winter, has
" produced two fuch illuſtrious men."

* Perhaps William.

"mous in the Benedictine order. John
"Pilfey reports that he found out the art
"of flying. But he says that projector
"never had the good fortune to get above a
"hundred and twenty yards at a time.
"However, no person else ever did so
"much."

In my next paper I will continue you some more of what Feyjoo says with regard to the English nation. At least, it shews you the idea the Spaniards hold us in.

LETTER XXXVIII.

SEVILLE, MAY 31, 1759.

AND now to continue you what Feyjoo says with regard to the English nation. His works continue to entertain me exceedingly.

" In phyfics, England has given more
" original authors than all other nations
" put together. Even the French, not-
" withftanding their zeal for the credit of
" their nation, confefs the Englifh to have
" the advantage over them in philofophical
" talents. I may fay without rafhnefs, that
" whatever advances have been made in
" phyfics this laft century, they have been
" all owing to chancellor Bacon. It was
" he who broke through the narrow bounds

within

" within which philosophy was confined
" till his time. It was he who threw down
" the columns upon which the *non plus ultra*
" with regard to natural knowlege had been
" engraved for so many ages. The learned
" Peter Gassendi was nothing but a faithful
" disciple of Bacon. What he had said in
" short, Gassendi repeated in his excellent
" philosophical writings in a more extended
" manner. What Descartes has worth any
" thing in his works, was all taken from
" Bacon. After him comes Boyle, and
" the most subtle Sir Isaac Newton, who
" were also great originals, not to mention
" Locke and Digby, and a great many
" others. But the liveliness of their genius
" has been attended with a misfortune
" which Bacon himself remarked. For
" since they once abandoned the true path
" with regard to religion, the greater life
" their reasoning has, the quicker they
" bewilder themselves. However, a Sir
" Thomas Moore has not been wanting to
" that

" that island, since heresy deformed it, a
" man no less famous for his learning than
" for his firmness in the catholic religion.
" Besides what I have already said, I have
" remarked that the English in their philo-
" sophical works give you an open explica-
" tion and free narrative, void of all artifice,
" of what they have found in their experi-
" ments, a thing which is not so frequently
" to be met with amongst authors of other
" nations. Particularly, it is a pleasure to
" see in Bacon, Boyle, and Sir Isaac New-
" ton, as well as in Sydenham the physi-
" cian, how, without boasting they tell
" you what they know, and without blush-
" ing confess what they are ignorant of.
" This is the very characteristic of sublime
" geniuses. What a pity, that the fatal
" cloud of heresy should overwhelm them
" with such melancholy darkness,"

These are all the remarks Feyjoo makes in an essay of his, entitled an intellectual chart

chart of the whole world. In a private letter to a friend he continues the subject a little, in which he attempts to recant what he had spoken in praise of the English nation. After having said that all arts and sciences have been continually migrating about the world, and that all nations either have or will enjoy them, he adds.

" These reflections make me now doubt
" of the idea I used to hold before, of a
" certain nation being superior to all the
" rest of Europe in intellectual perspicacity.
" But why should I be afraid to name it?
" I speak of the English nation. With
" regard to the modern English, there is a
" palpable reason why there ought to be
" more great men among them in natural
" knowledge than in any other nation
" whatever, and yet without their exceeding
" others in natural genius. The reason is that
" they apply themselves more, or, at least,
" more commonly to study. Monsr. Rolin,

"so well known in the world by the many
"and good histories he has written, confess-
"es with some grief that the application, we
"are speaking, of reigns infinitely more in
"England than in France. He knew this
"by having conversed with a great many
"gentlemen of that nation, upon their
"travels. He says, he hardly ever saw one
"of them who was not adorned with ex-
"cellent knowledge in one or more facul-
"ties. And I have been informed from
"other quarters, that a great many lords
"or principal gentlemen, if not the greatest
"part, have excellent libraries, which they
"make use of as well themselves, as permit
"others to do the same. So that it is very
"probable that England, without having
"any particular advantage in natural ta-
"lents, may have persons better instructed
"in arts and sciences than other nations.
"One field, without being of a richer qua-
"lity, will produce more than another by
"its being cultivated better. Besides, it is
"more

"more easy to find four persons of remark-
"able genius among four thousand that
"apply themselves to study, than among
"two thousand."

LETTER XXXIX.

SEVILLE, JUNE 5, 1759.

FEYJOO goes on as follows in his letter upon the English nation. Tho' there are some things pretty nearly the same as what I gave you in the quotation taken from the essay of his, entitled The intellectual Chart of the World, I will give you what he writes at full length.

" True it is that England has exhibited so
" many great geniuses, and of so superior a
" stamp, as to have induced various literati
" of other nations to acknowledge some ad-
" vantage in their understanding above the
" rest. Heideger, a German author, says
" he found in the English a more subtle ge-
" nius than in all other nations. The great
" Fontenelle (than whom no person was
" more

" more capable of deciding this queſtion)
" altho' he does not expreſsly ſay the ſame
" in any part of his works, yet in many he
" ſpeaks with ſuch emphaſis of the talents
" of the Engliſh, that without any violence
" we may judge him to be of the ſame opi-
" nion. What is very remarkable, is, that
" there are a great many French authors,
" who notwithſtanding the noted emulation
" between the two nations, give it for grant-
" ed that the Engliſh beat them in penetra-
" tion and in depth of thinking, reſerving,
" however, to themſelves the glory of ex-
" plaining their thoughts better. And in-
" deed it is not to be denied in this that the
" French greatly ſurpaſs thoſe neighbours
" of theirs ; ſo that it is almoſt a proverb to
" ſay, Engliſh ideas with a Frenchman's
" pen.

" Father Rapin, with regard to this ſub-
" ject, merits a particular conſideration above
" all other French authors, not only as be-
" ing

"ing a very famous critic upon the writers
"of his nation, as well as those of others,
"but also upon account of his great devo-
"tion, which would naturally incline him
"to regard with displeasure the daringness
"of the genius of the English, as treading
"under foot the most assured maxims upon
"which our religion is founded. Notwith-
"standing this he does not fail to do justice
"to their talents with regard to penetration
"and depth of thought in philosophy. In
"the 18th section of his reflections upon
"philosophy, after confessing this in gene-
"ral, he expresses the advantage the Eng-
"lish have with regard to penetration by
"calling it, 'that depth of genius common
"to their nation.' Coming afterwards to
"speak in particular of original modern
"philosophers, he says, he finds but one in
"France, which is Descartes, one in Italy,
"viz. Galileo, but that in England he counts
"to the number of three, Bacon, Hobbes
"and Boyle.

"What

"What would father Rapin have said,
"if he had lived to behold that won-
"der of understanding, he who with more
"than eagle's flight mounted to the celestial
"spheres, and with eyes more piercing than
"those of the lynx, appears to have pene-
"trated the depth of those abysses. Much
"more than all this is expressed by the name
"of the great Newton. Of the three men-
"tioned by father Rapin I have never seen
"Hobbes, nor any of the least of his works.
"I know also that he is detested for his im-
"piety. A man who attempted to deprive
"the king of heaven of his divinity, to
"invest with it the kings of the earth, not
"owning other laws, divine or human, than
"the mere will of princes.

"Bacon and Boyle were original and pro-
"found philosophers; Newton still more so
"than either of them. To Bacon nature
"gave the entrance into her magnificent pa-
"lace, unfolding to his sight the gates
"which

"which led to her moſt inmoſt receſſes.
" And he acquainted the world with what he
" had diſcovered in his two famous works,
" Novum Organum Scientiarum, and that
" de augmentis Scientiarum. To Boyle
" ſhe delivered the key of one of thoſe
" principal gates, through which he en-
" tered into the hall where inanimate bo-
" dies were anatomized *(a droll expreſſion)*.
" To Newton ſhe gave a bright torch, by
" the light of which he was able to regiſter
" the ample ſpaces of that great edifice,
" where former philoſophers had met with
" nothing but darkneſs. I could name a
" great many other remarkable perſonages
" belonging to England, but ſuch as are to
" be paralleled in other nations. Now my
" purpoſe was not to produce to the public
" all the great men, but only thoſe few,

" ————Qui ob facta ingentia poſſunt
" Vere homines, et ſemi-dei, heroeſque vocari."

What

What Englishman can read this, and when he considers it as published in the centre of Spain, not be proud of the character his nation bears there? I confess I think myself a greater man than I was before I perused it, and I make no doubt but these treatises of Feyjoo will help to banish from the Spanish soil those clouds of ignorance which have hitherto oppressed a very sensible nation.

LETTER XL.

SEVILLE, JUNE 14, 1759.

I will still make you cut another letter with a continuation of Feyjoo, who goes on thus.

" Notwithstanding what I have said, the
" reason alledged before, of the English na-
" tion's applying more to the cultivation of
" letters than other kingdoms, is still suffi-
" cient to make us doubt, whether those
" giant authors I have pointed out, may not
" be rather owing to that, than to any parti-
" cular native disposition in the inhabitants
" of the island of Great Britain. To this
" we may add, that the genius of the Eng-
" lish being more hardy and intrepid than
" that of other nations, contributes much
" to

" to the splendor and credit of their pro-
" ductions. Certain it is, that in two per-
" sons of equal talents, one however, of a
" timid, and the other of a daring dispofi-
" tion, the latter will outshine the former,
" not only in common conversation, in
" which a little impudence is of particular
" advantage, but even as an author. A
" timid genius, tho' on many occasions,
" perhaps, capable of rising above the com-
" mon way of thinking and reasoning of
" mankind, yet contains himself within
" such narrow bounds, from dangers his
" imagination paints to him in committing
" to writing any particular ideas, that
" sometimes where he might aspire to the
" glory of an original, fear damps his
" flight, and he remains buried among the
" endless multitude of vulgar writers. On
" the contrary, he who is not afraid of
" launching out into the open ocean in
" spight of what storms may break upon
" his head, by giving freely to the world

U " those

" thofe thoughts which an elevated genius
" may fuggeft, is known and efteemed by
" men of underftanding for what he is.
" Courage and underftanding muft be united
" together to make heroes as well in literary
" enterprifes as in thofe of war, at leaft, to
" make people known for such.

" But from this laft reflection an argu-
" ment of parity may be deduced in favor
" of the common opinion, which gives to
" different nations unequal geniufes. If
" the Englifh are more courageous than the
" inhabitants of other kingdoms, it follows
" that courage is in a greater or lefs degree
" in different climates, which without
" doubt muft arife from the different con-
" ftitutions of the people. From this dif-
" ference in their conftitutions, to follow
" the moft current opinion, which does not
" admit any effential inequality in fouls,
" arifes the difference of genius. That their
" conftitutions are different is to be collected
" not

" not only from one perſon ſurpaſſing ano-
" ther in valor, but alſo from the difference
" that is found in their various inclinations
" and temper, which undeniably ariſes from
" conſtitution. One nation is more active,
" another more idle; one more choleric,
" another more patient; one more open
" like the French, another more circum-
" ſpect like the Spaniards; one more ſincere
" like the Flemiſh nation, and another
" more cautious like the Italians, &c.

" To ſay the truth, I cannot ſolve this
" argument ſo ſatisfactorily as not to leave
" room for replies upon replies. As the
" anſwering all theſe would take up too
" much time, I think it beſt to elude their
" force, and only balance the caſe with a
" contrary argument taken from experience.
" I have lived from my youth in a republic,
" namely, that of the college of my order,
" where there is a continual exact examina-
" tion of the perſons that compoſe it, to

"the end that they may be advanced in
"literary employments, or excluded from
"them. And even after employments have
"been conferred upon individuals, the nice
"obfervations we make of thofe who fill
"their offices beft, and fhew fuperior or
"inferior talents in the exercife of their
"profeffion, may permit us to fay that by
"regular degrees we are daily weighing the
"value of their refpective intellectual abili-
"ties. Now in the fixty-one years and
"above that I have lived in this community,
"I have feen fubjects without number in-
"troduced into it from all the provinces
"of our monarchy, fo that I have been
"able to found tolerably well the equality
"or inequality of the perfons that came
"from them with regard to the difcuffion
"in hand. But I declare, tho' this has
"been many times the object of my thoughts,
"I could never difcover any fuperiority that
"thofe of one province had in genius over
"any other. However, you may find a
"pretty

"pretty remarkable difference in their turn. But it does not follow from thence that their talents are unequal.

"I have here given you what has prefented itfelf on both fides the queftion, as things occurred to me, without any premeditated order. I now imagine you will afk me what is my determination? Is there any nation fuperior in natural talents to the reft or no? What I anfwer is, that the cafe feems fo dubious to me that I dare not pronounce the verdict. I will conform myfelf to what you determine concerning it. Heaven guard you, &c."

I am juft returned from a little expedition I have made to a place called the *Rocio*. If I have nothing more entertaining for my next paper, I may give you fome of the particulars of it. There are prodigious quantities of people go to this place once a year

year to adore an image of the Virgin Mary, and as it is fituated in the middle of a foreft, with no houfe near it but a little hermitage, and the church, they live the two days they always confume in this act of devotion in arbours made for that purpofe, which, together with their continual finging, dancing, playing upon the guitar and other inftruments, made a moft rural fcene. At night too there were not bad fireworks, but perhaps more of this hereafter.

LET.

LETTER XLI.

SEVILLE, JUNE 18, 1759.

I Will now, as I have promised, give you some circumstances of my queer jaunt to the Virgin Mary del *Rocio*, or of the *Dew*, which I spoke to you about.

My companion the vice-consul being ready, and our horses at the door, I took leave of my landlord Don Ignatio de la Portela, and set forth. I need not tell you that Andalusian horses are very famous, not for speed, for in that perhaps ours and those of Barbary excel, but for their great docility and beautiful warlike make. Thrown over my left shoulder lay my cloak, a constant attendant upon a Spaniard in all his peregrinations. We were stopt soon after our setting

setting out by a prodigious concourse of people gathered together to see eighty-eight redeemed captives enter the city. They were just come from Barbary, and had been redeemed by the subscriptions of charitable persons, aided by the king of Spain's bounty. There were two Irish Roman catholics among them, as likewise two women, a great many boys, and one Moor escaped from his native country with the intention of becoming a christian, but the ceremony is to be deferred till he gets to Madrid, where it is to be performed I think with some pomp. They were all dressed in white cloaks, with the badge of their redemption fastened upon them. In other respects they still retained their Moorish habits, and the oldest had long venerable beards, for some of them had been a number of years in captivity. I spoke to one of the Irishmen, who had been taken not long before on board a Spanish vessel. He said that his principal employment during his slavery was carrying

ing stones to build a mosque. They say the Spaniards have now no more of their subjects prisoners in Africa. The vice-consul and myself having at last extricated ourselves from this tumult, we got to the bridge and passed Triano, which, indeed, is only a kind of suburb to Seville. The first village in our way to La Puebla, where we were to lie that night, was San Juan de Alfarache, very pleasantly situated upon a rising hill, and not at a great distance from the river Guadalquivir. We had some rain, which was followed by a cold wind, unexperienced they say in this part of the world so late in the season, and more penetrating, perhaps, than any felt in England. After a very disagreeable ride, we got to La Puebla, and hired a cart in which to proceed upon our journey the next morning. You may wonder to hear me talk of such a vehicle, and especially when I inform you it was to be drawn by oxen; but we must have gone either in this manner or on horseback, and

the

the latter would have been very inconvenient upon many accounts, particularly as we fhould in that cafe have had no where to lie; whereas, a tilted cart, with good mattraffes under us, made a moft commodious bed, for in the place where we were going, as I have already hinted, there were no houfes. The church in which the image of the Virgin Mary of the *Dew* ftands, is fituated in the middle of a foreft, where the beft accommodations you can get are under arbours made on purpofe, which are not fo convenient as tilted carts, and many perfons come in them upon that account. * * *

* * * * * * * * * * * *

LETTER XLII.

SEVILLE, JUNE 22, 1759.

ABOUT two o'clock in the morning the vice-conful and myfelf mounted our ignoble vehicle, where extending ourfelves upon the mattraffes, we foon were lulled to fleep by the flow and fedate motion of our cloven-footed animals.

There is one advantage in thefe Spanifh carts, which is, that there is no danger of being overturned, as the axle-tree is twice as broad as any ever yet made in England. What is their reafon for this I know not, but it certainly looks very particular, efpecially as the carriage is in general not broader than ours. We arrived at breakfaft at a pretty little village, where we were regaled by fome of the vice-conful's acquaintances. They gave

gave us bread daubed over with a fort of fyrup, which added to fome tolerably good wine compleated our repaft. Our cattle having by this time grazed fufficiently before the door of our hofts, were once more yoked to the carriage, tho' to yoke is an improper expreffion, as the Spaniards make their oxen draw by their foreheads, bearing the weight of the pole or fhaft juft behind their horns. They have but one fhaft which comes out from the middle of the cart, and is croffed at the end by a kind of fplinter bar, that lies upon their heads. I will not venture to fay whether the Spaniards or we are in the right, but they certainly ought to know where the principal ftrength of thefe animals lies, upon account of their frequent bullfeafts, in which cruel exercife all nations allow them to be extremely dextrous. At prefent, indeed, there is neither that diverfion nor any other, upon account of the prefent diforder of the king of Spain, who is not expected to live, and is reported to be out of

his

his mind. However, you may often fee a little fpecimen of dexterity of this kind in the fields, where the country people make no difficulty of provoking a bull and playing with him. The chief foundation they ground this art upon is the knowing that a bull fome little time before he ftrikes fhuts his eyes, fo that by agility and practice, with the help of their cloak, by which they deceive him in flipping a ftep or two befide it, and holding it out to the extent of their arm, there is not much danger of any accident happening. *

* * * * * * * * * * *

LETTER XLIII.

SEVILLE, JUNE 27, 1759.

BEING set out from the little village where we breakfasted, we proceeded with the usual gravity of our ruminating animals to Villa Manriques to dinner, where the vice-consul knew almost the whole town, which occupied us in making twenty visits at least. I believe there were fifty carts like ours here, all engaged in the same expedition, and all their passengers seemed determined to be as merry as they could. The guitars were resounding, while the people danced all about the streets. To give you some idea of the rural dances of the Andalusians, I shall only say to you what a sea captain swore to me, that they exactly resemble what he had seen upon the coast of Guinea. But I think he was too hard upon our manner of dancing here, for tho' there is certainly not much grace in it, yet there is something pastoral and pleasing, especially in the women with their castaignets and tambourines. The former is a little wooden machine, which makes a sort of noise like a rattle by closing it, and is held in each hand; the latter is only a flat drum, with gingling pieces of tin hanging round it. The manner of dress too among the countrymen is pretty. In most towns the cloak I have mentioned so often to you is worn, but in the country it very frequently gives place to a short jacquet put over their waistcoat, from which it is always of a different colour, and the sleeves, instead of covering their arms, hang down genteelly behind. I do not, however, think this dress looks well but upon young people. After having dined at Villa Manriques, we proceeded to an old hunting palace belonging to the king of Spain, situated at the beginning of the forest, in which the *Rocio*, where we were going, lies,

lies, tho' at the diſtance of ſome leagues. We all had free acceſs into this royal manſion, in conſequence of which, it was filled in a little time by our fellow travellers; and as the carts came thronging along very thick after each other, we ſoon made up a formidable aſſembly. The diverſion was ſinging and dancing till the ſun was ſet, when on all hands fires were lighted abroad under the adjacent trees, and different ſuppers prepared by each reſpective community. About ten o'clock our whole caravan ſet out afreſh, and towards ſun-riſe we arrived at the ſcene of diverſion. I confeſs, the ruralneſs and novelty of the thing ſtruck me. The ſeeing ſo many thouſand people all at once, dreſſed ſo paſtorally, and lying about under the trees, preſented no leſs than a ſecond Arcadia to my view. The ſound of their guitars and other muſical inſtruments greatly heightened the idea of ancient ſtories of ſhepherds and ſhepherdeſſes. We ſtayed all that night, and till twelve o'clock the

next

next day, to fee the concluding proceffion of the image of the Virgin Mary, which certainly was not worth the time we loft. All being at laft over, we returned with much company and mufic, and much in the fame manner we came from Seville. As we were dining the next day under fome trees, ftill attended by many people, a wag was paffing by quickly on horfeback, who being afked by fome of the men whither he was going in fuch hafte, replied, that he was carrying *horns* to Seville. The words were no fooner out of his mouth than away he galloped, and was in the right to do fo, as the whole company got up in a rage, and began pelting him with ftones, fome of which were near ftriking the fugitive infulter. It is wonderful what an effect the fimple word *horns* has upon an Andalufian, and it is faid, that if you call one a *cabron* or goat, nothing can fave your life but flight. This feems to be fome remains of the old Spanifh jealoufy, for in other countries people do not attribute so extraordinary a force to these words, without, indeed, they were intended as an insult by the pronouncer of them.

I could have made a longer description of this religious merry-making, and of the fireworks, and other entertainments we had, but imagine you are sick of it already.

LETTER XLIV.

Seville, July 6, 1759.

I Will now give you some account of a little journey I have made to Palma, not that any thing remarkable happened in it, but the sending you these descriptions affords me an opportunity of enlarging upon the customs and manners of the Andalusians more agreeably, perhaps, than if I was dryly to tell you them without any narration. In all cases you are by bargain to be contented with what I send you.

I set out in company with an Irish gentleman and one Rodriguez, who came with us to take care of the horses. We had been so long detained upon account of their not coming at the time appointed, that we imagined we should have been broiled alive by setting out so late. A gentle wind, however, in our faces, mitigated the heat of the sun till we arrived at the *Venta* or country inn where we were to dine, about three leagues from Seville. A Spanish league is four good English miles, so that we had gone at least twelve. We here dismounted, and Rodriguez conducted the horses into the stable, where he gave them plenty of straw to feed upon. They had, likewise, some barley, which here supplies the place of oats, but chopt straw is the only exchange they have for hay. The heat of these countries is, I imagine, the reason they have nothing better for their cattle, as all grass is parched up long before this time, and the country would now afford very little green if it were not for the olive trees and vineyards. But what to me seems particular is, that, tho' our horses in England eat as much hay as they please, besides other things, and have always clean straw to lie upon, yet they look in general leaner, much

more

more coarse grained, and much less beautiful than those of Spain. Perhaps the climate, and their not willingly making them sweat, may be some assistance. Not that I think a sportsman would at all approve of a Spanish horse, as they would make but a bad figure in the chase. However, upon the whole I can not but allow them to be very fine animals. The majesticalness of their shape and gait, added to their great docility and meekness, tho' without want of spirit, makes it a pleasure to ride them. And yet a great many lie only upon their own dung, and eat little more than straw. In a campaign they would have great advantages over British cavalry, that has been nursed up more delicately. There is another property the Spaniards cry up in their horses, which is that of never kicking. How true the assertion may be I know not, all I am certain of is, that I have never seen them strike, and yet the Spaniards are very familiar in walking about their heels. If by any extraordinary chance a horse should happen to lift up his legs, they with great gravity affirm it to be owing to his being of a bastard race; for, say they, no true Spanish horse could ever do such a thing. The reason Spanish horses are so little seen out of the kingdom is, that it is death for any person to attempt to export them without a particular privilege from the court, which, I believe, is very hard to obtain. But horses are smuggled into Portugal, as I think I have already told you that the Spaniards are reckoned the boldest in that way of any nation. But to conclude my equestrian dissertation, and convey you once more to the inn our steeds were then at. It was, indeed, more calculated for the reception of such animals, than of human beings; however, we got there some of the best olives I ever eat in all my life. With these and the provision we brought with us, we made out a very good dinner, and after a gentle sleep to digest it, set out for Carmona, a large city

city to which we arrived at fun-fet. As Carmona is fituated upon an eminence, it is much cooler than Seville, which ftands in a hole by the river-fide, like an Englifh town. To enjoy then a little the frefh air, which was breathing through the ftreets, and to fee what fort of a place we were got to, my friend and I fallied out of our inn, leaving word with Rodriguez to buy fome eggs, and get them dreffed for fupper (meagre fare!) After we had walked about the city for fome time, we went out at one of the gates of it, and fat ourfelves down upon the ridge of the hill on which Carmona ftands. We here ftayed fome time invoking the propitious gales to arife and fan us,

Aura veni, pectufque intra gratiffima noftrum.

Nor were the gentle gales inattentive to our defire. From the valley beneath us fprung up a breeze, which renewed our fpirits, unbraced before by the too great heat of the weather. The valley below us might be, be, I believe, seven or eight Spanish leagues in circumference, and was sowed with different kinds of grain, most part of which was then reaping, as you will easily imagine the harvests are much forwarder here than with us. The business of a reaper in this climate is surely most terrible. To stand with their faces for so many hours bent towards the ground, now burning with the too powerful rays of the sun, seems enough to kill any person. Some, indeed, they say, in reality drop down dead, and that all would do the same, if it was not owing to a mess the country people make among themselves of garlick, vinegar, and some other ingredients, which they hold as a preservative against heat.

LETTER XLV.

SEVILLE, JULY 9, 1759.

NOT to keep you any longer at Carmona, (for the many repetitions of my fare and inns cannot but be tirefome) I will only tell you we fet out from it after having paffed a very bad night upon account of the quantity of vermin. They are one of the plagues of all hot countries, but I think they are worfe in Spain than Italy. We are much peftered here by a fort of gnat, called in England mufkatoes, from a corruption of the Spanifh word *mofquitos*, which are very venomous and difagreeable. Juft without the gate of the town we arrived to a very fteep defcent, which leads into the valley I mentioned in my laft, and which we were now to crofs. It was, I believe, about two or three leagues over; but the heat we fuffered made that

diftance

distance appear double. Having at length passed it, and a village called Campana, with which it terminates, we came into a country less broiling indeed, but much more barren. It was a sort of ground the Spaniards call Palmares, upon account of little low thickets of palms growing all about it, not much thicker nor higher, nor very different in resemblance, from our fern-brakes in England. Where these heathy plants grow they say that cultivation is of no use, as the soil is naturally unfruitful. This uncomfortable desert face of the country continued till we came near Palma, where the appearance of things was a little more smiling, as at least there was here and there some cultivation, but still it might be called rather desert, and continued so till we came to the banks of the river Henil, or as the Spaniards write it Xenil, which runs just under Palma. We were here obliged to stay a long time in the burning sun for a ferry boat, and when we got up to Palma, which was on fire, if I may be be allowed the expreſſion, were a long time before we could accommodate ourſelves with a quarter, or ſeparate room. We had nothing but the remainder of a ham to dine upon, as no freſh proviſion can reſiſt theſe great heats. After our ſalt repaſt, the heat inclined us much to ſleep. But to our misfortune, there were no beds, and the floor was ſo uncleanably dirty, that we did not care to lay ourſelves down upon it. The beſt method we thought we could take was the following. We went into the ſtable and cleaned enough of the range of mangers for us two to lie in. To make our bed the ſofter, we took all the ſtraw our horſes could eat from that time till our departure, and laid it under us. As it was already chopped for conſumption, it proved but a prickly kind of mattraſs, tho' I ſlept very found upon it, till an impertinent jack-aſs, drawn, I ſuppoſe, by the odour of the ſtraw, began treating me very roughly with his ſnout. Thus diſcompoſed I got up, and was retiring into our room, when a very droll quarrel between Rodriguez and another man detained me. This latter was the master of the jack-afs that had diſturbed me, and who had a good many other animals of the ſame ſpecies now in the ſtable. The poor beaſts, urged by hunger, for perhaps they had eaten nothing all that day, and ſeeing that our three horſes were plentifully ſupplied with barley, which Rodriguez had juſt given them, the poor jack-aſſes beholding with invidious eye this cruel diſtinction, having been for ſome time melancholy ſpectators of it, could no longer refrain from intruding, and becoming partakers likewiſe of the good fare. Rodriguez ſeeing their familiarity, accoſted their maſter with a very civil deportment, and without any ſeeming paſſion. "Do you know, ſir," ſays he, "that if your beaſts eat our corn, I ſhall cer- "tainly take up that piece of wood which lies "there, and knock their brains out?" To which the other anſwered, that with regard

to

to that he might do as he pleafed, " but do
" you know, fir," adds he very civilly likewife,
" that if you do, I may chance afterwards to
" take up the fame piece of wood, and knock
" your brains out too ?" Now each began to
fwell, and in all likelihood the bufinefs
would not have blown over without a fray,
had not my friend interpofed his authority,
and brought the antagonifts to terms of
peace. However, Rodriguez could not help
grumbling for a long time after. " If," fays
he, " the fellow had come and taken my
" victuals from me, there would have been
" nothing in it, or even if his horfes had
" eat the provender of my horfes, but that
" his jack-affes fhould come and ferve my
" horfes fo, is not to be borne."

I give you this trifling anecdote as it illuf-
trates a little the character of the common
Andalufians, and indeed there is a ftriking
refemblance between many of them and
Sancho

Sancho Pança, which, however is not at all wonderful, as Cervantes drew his pictures from nature as much as any of the characters in Tom Jones are drawn.

The morning we had come out Rodriguez complained much of hunger, and told us the nice air which then blew had entirely digested his last night's supper, thereby archly hinting to us that he had eat no breakfast at all that morning. He then was as desirous of opening the wallet he bore upon his horse as Sancho was, but we prevailed upon him to refrain till we came to the Venta, where we dined.

LETTER XLVI.

SEVILLE, JULY 12, 1759.

I WILL paſs over what happened to us during our ſtay at Palma, as the time was moſtly employed in viſiting, ſeeing proceſſions and being regaled with ſweetmeats. One morning, indeed, we rode out to ſee a little of the country. We went down towards the river Henil, which we had paſſed in coming, and along the ſide of which there are a great number of fruit gardens, for Palma furniſhes a great part of the neighbouring country with fruit, which, indeed, is the only ſort of commerce they have. Fruit gardens in this country are always ſituated upon the banks of rivers, or in places where they can have plenty of water, as otherwiſe they would be burnt up by the ſun. They have different kinds of engines

engines which convey their water in pretty little neat rills to every part of the garden. One of them called a *noria* feems to be the cheapeft, moft fimple, and, therefore, the beft of the kind I ever met with, merely pitchers faftened to a great perpendicular wheel turned by a horizontal one. After having been about a great many of thefe gardens, gathering the fruit from the trees as we rode along, (for none begrudge plumbs, pears, or apples in this plentiful fruit climate), we went to another fpot about two miles from where we then were, to fee the place where the Henil and Guadalquivir unite their ftreams and form but one river, which goes on afterwards by the name of the latter, and under that denomination proceeds to Seville, and fo on to the fea at St. Lucar. It was a pretty place enough, but the heat begun to be fo ftrong that we were glad to get to our inn, which accordingly we did in lefs than an hour after. * * * * * * * *
* * * * * * * * * * * *

LET-

LETTER XLVII.

SEVILLE, JULY 16, 1759.

IN my former letter I said it would be tiresome to give you an exact description of every thing we did at Palma. Let it suffice that there we passed our time in seeing processions and making visits, for the inhabitants treated us with much civility. As we resolved in our return to go to Carmona by dinner, we sat out very early in the morning. Our breakfast was under a tree, with our horses turned to graze *a la Española*. We were much distressed for water, which seems more difficult sometimes to get at in these countries than wine, nor could we find any till we came to Campana, the village which stands upon the farther edge of the valley of Carmona. Notwithstanding the haste we made, time had run on so fast that the sun was burning hot when we entered the low ground, and to delay us more I found my horse wanted a couple of shoes, so that we were forced to go a foot pace quite to the town. In ascending the hill, just before you arrive at Carmona, the very earth seemed to send forth flames; but at last we entered the gate, and soon after the inn, with no small joy. As we had now very little provision we were obliged to make out our dinner with eggs, fruit, and other things we could buy, and our after-dinner's sleep being finished, we set out in the cool of the evening for the desolate inn three leagues from Seville Here with no better bed than a table with my cloak round me, I reposed till sun-rise, when we set out again and got to Seville before the heat could much affect us.

To fill up my present paper, I will give you an inscription that is written upon the gate of an hospital in this town, which I have literally translated from the Spanish. Perhaps

Perhaps you may not understand it; however, it will strongly mark the bigotted ideas of the nation I am at present with. Indeed I think it a master-piece of enthusiasm, and if ever you have occasion to make any inscription you may extract the substance from this.

It is as follows.

"This work of the infirmaries of the "hospital of the holy charity was finished "with the perfection and greatness with "which they are now seen, in the year of "our safety 1674.

"Our Lord Jesus Christ being ruler in "Heaven; he being high pontiff of the "church, who is the high priest according "to the order of Melchisedec.

"He who reigns in Heaven reigning in "the Spains, his divine majesty being the "eldest-brother of this holy house, and he
"who

" who commands in Heaven, being a poor
" infirm in thefe beds, which were made
" at the coft and expence of the moft high
" God his father, with whom he lives and
" reigns in unity with the Holy Ghoft be-
" yond all ages."

LETTER XLVIII.

SEVILLE, JULY 26, 1759.

I SHALL fet out fhortly for Cadiz and Gibraltar, and am only waiting for a letter I expect from Lifbon. In the interval I will give you fome particulars of another little journey I have made to Cabral.

I fet out with the fame Irifh gentleman and in much the fame form as we had done for Palma. We dined at Carmona, but left our former road when we had defcended into the valley. The next morning we abandoned a miferable inn that had houfed us for the night and got to Ecija, a large city, by a little after fun-rife. Our inn ftood juft by the bridge, and facing it a gigantic ftatue of St. Chriftopher. The river running by the Ecija is the Henil, which I made

made you acquainted with in my former journey. This town is situated in a hole with naked hills all round it something like Winchester. It is reckoned the hottest place in all Spain, and upon that account is called the frying-pan of Andalusia.

We were greatly benighted in getting from Ecija to the solitary hovel which was to receive us that evening. Our best bed was upon some flint stones, at the door of the inn in the open air, where we slept for an hour or two till our horses had done their corn. Nothing can be a greater proof of the fineness of this climate than to see the people sleeping about on the bare ground with nothing but the heavens to cover them. It would be almost death in England, but in this very dry country I do not think there is any thing very unwholesome in it. It is now several months since we have had a drop of rain, nor is any expected till towards the month of October, when the

heats

heats begin to ceafe. There are but very little dews neither, quite the contrary of Italy, where you may fometimes fee the evening dew defcending like a fmall rain. This may be the caufe of many parts in Italy being fo very unhealthy, that they fay it is fatal to fleep a night in them. However as, notwithftanding the drynefs of the air, we were not very content with our ftony couch, we mounted our horfes as foon as they were able to proceed, and about three hours after day break arrived at Cabral.

The country about this place is exceffively pretty, and refembles Italy more than Spain. Hills, wood and water variegate the fcene in a moft delightful manner, while a rugged mountain impendent over the town adds to the romanticnefs of the view. Cabral itfelf is like other country towns, tho' cleaner than moft I have feen in Spain, and it has the advantage of having little rivulets running through almoft all the ftreets, a thing

very

very agreeable in this hot climate; not that the heat is so oppressive here as in Seville, the neighbourhood of a very mountainous country towards Grenada rendering the air much fresher. Our time passed as at Palma, in visiting and seeing the country. A canon of Grenada was our principal conductor. He one evening carried us to one of the prettiest water-falls I ever saw, where we sat down on the grass and entertained ourselves with the agreeableness of the place, till the sun had verged pretty near to the horizon. We then began walking on afresh, and went to the foot of the mountain impending over Cabral. From a cleft in it issued two pretty little cool rivulets, which afterwards unite their streams and form a small river, called by the name of the town, till it loses both itself and denomination in the Henil. Under the shadow of this mountain and straggling along the sides of the rivulets, whose banks were of living rock, sat a number of gentlemen and ladies enjoying the *fresco* this delicious

licious place afforded. As we were dry we went to the opening whence one of the streams broke forth from the heart of the mountain, and having borrowed a glafs of one of the gentlemen, drank plentifully of the refrefhing liquor, as it was not inferior in coolnefs to that tempered by fnow in houfes, nor in fweetnefs to the fineft water you ever tafted. You may wonder to hear me talk fo delicioufly, and fo much in praife of a beverage rarely ufed by the fubjects of Great Britain, but the Spaniards drink very little of any thing elfe, and, indeed, heat certainly renders every ftrong liquid difagreeable. We fupped that night with the canon, where an old maid fervant, who, I fuppofe, had never ftirred out of the place, pleafed me mightily. She feemed very much furprized at the bad Spanifh I talked, and not being able to contain herfelf any longer, " What!" exclaims fhe, " and don't they talk " the fame *there* * as *here* ?" The innocence with

---

* Allà como aqui.

with which she said this added a particular grace to her ignorance, and upon our answering her that *there* they talked a quite different language from what they did *here*, she broke out into an exclamation of wonder at the odd things which happen in this world. Our supper being finished with the canon, we retired to our inn, not without casting an envious eye upon a large mat which lay in his room, and which would have proved a much better bed than those we were to expect.

LETTER XLIX.

SEVILLE, AUGUST 5, 1759.

I WILL conclude my Cabral expedition in a few lines, not to tire you with repetitions. The rest of our time was spent much in the same manner as what I have described. At last setting out in the evening and baiting at our old hovel, where I had lain upon the flints, we got in very good time to Ecija the next morning. We again set out from thence towards the evening, not for Carmona, the road we came, but for Marchena, which we knew was a shorter way, and the people of the inn at Ecija assured us we could not mistake it. We did not, however, arrive there without many perils and dangers of roads and robbers. The following morning after an easy ride we arrived at Seville in good time.

I have

I have been this morning to see a giant, who has exhibited himself to a great part of Europe. He is surprisingly tall, I dare not say how much, but withal seems equally weak and unhappy. I did not know the difficulties of a giant traveller till he recounted them to me. No bed to lie in but out of which your feet extend a considerable way. No coach to ride in, but where you are obliged to sit bent double. Wearied with the posture, he was forced at times to take a little walk on foot, to the utter astonishment of the Spanish countrymen who met him, and fell prostrate in adoration of what they thought St. Christopher. Coming one festival day to a country village, he attended high mass, after which there was a sermon. The preacher, who had not observed him when he mounted the pulpit, is said to have no sooner cast his eyes upon this monstrous figure, then struck with amazement, he stopped short, sunk down, and was heard to repeat ejaculations at the bottom of his pulpit. But tho'

tho' this amazing man caufes terror to the vulgar, I felt myfelf touched with much compaffion towards him, and the more fo as he has fold himfelf for three years to the perfon who conducts him, and who hurries him about that he may make the more money. His gains, however, have been leffened here at Seville by the magiftrates obliging his gigantic ward to go and hear mafs, notwithftanding the reprefentations that were made of the great lofs it would be, if he was feen publicly at church. But the divines have determined that he is rather more than lefs of a chriftian by being a giant, and is, therefore, at leaft equally obliged with all other catholics to attend the duties of the church. A mafs, however, is prepared for him very early in the morning on holy days, but it does not prevent many people from getting up and feeing him gratis.

I intend next week to leave Seville and my friends here, who are moftly Irifh, fled, as they express it, from the tyrannical government of England. Whether their complaints are just or no, I cannot say, however, they tell you that all their offices are given away to the English, whose only merit is a servile flattery to courtiers. They complain likewise greatly of persecution with regard to religion, tho' I should think without justice. The law that no Roman catholic can serve in any public capacity is by them cried down as impolitic. What numbers, say they, of our countrymen who now serve France and Spain and other foreign nations, would have devoted themselves to the defence of their native country, if the rigor of the laws had not hindered 'persons of their persuasion from being employed under the British government. They likewise complain of not being allowed to wear swords, or ride a horse of above five pounds value, laws which they say are put into execution.

This

This is what they complain of, which I leave you to interpret as you think beſt. One or two Engliſhmen there are among them, but as they are *Iriſhified* I ſhall not diſtinguiſh them from the ſame claſs.

LETTER L.

SEVILLE, AUGUST 16, 1759.

I SHALL not leave Seville till the 20th, and have nothing elfe at prefent to inform you of, but that the vice-conful who accompanied me to the *Rocio* died yefterday morning and was buried this. His death is attributed to the having made a journey this very hot weather to fome quickfilver mines there are in this country. They are reckoned very noxious, and might be rendered ftill worfe by the prefent heat of the fun, which a feacaptain declared to me yefterday was more furious than in Jamaica. Thefe mines are fo peftilential that no perfon, they fay, is fent to work in them except condemned people, who feldom refift above a couple of years. But whatever was the caufe of the vice-conful's death, he certainly is no more,

for

for I was this morning at his burial. His corps I could not fee, for tho' it was expofed, there was fuch a ftench iffuing from it, that none could approach it, and yet he had been dead only four and twenty hours. A fign of the great heat of this country. But tho' it creates putrefaction eafily, it foon draws up the noxious effluvia of it, and the bodies of dead dogs and cats, which are thrown plentifully into the ftreets, are not offenfive the day after their being expofed, except to the eyes of the paffengers. All the Irifh attended the vice-conful's funeral, and formed a long proceffion, for he was a Roman catholic. But why fhould I talk to you of burials? You might like better, perhaps, that I fhould fpeak of life. I will do fo, and give you a remarkable example of it in a man formerly of Seville, and fo conclude my paper.

"Don Juan Remirez de Buftamente, na-
" tive of this city, lived to the age of one
" hundred

" hundred and twenty-one years. He was
" married five times, and by his wives had
" forty-two children, and by other women
" nine. He was a great failor, and knew
" feven Indian languages. At the age of
" ninety-nine years he was ordained prieft,
" and always faid mafs, and affifted in the
" quire of the parifh church of St. Loren-
" zo till his death, which was occafioned
" by a fall. He was buried in the fame
" church, the 30th of September 1678."

LETTER LI.

SEVILLE, AUGUST 19, 1759.

I THINK I can give you nothing more entertaining for this paper than an extract from the Madrid gazette.

" Madrid, 14th Auguft, 1759. On Friday
" the 10th of this month, at a quarter after
" four in the morning, the ills of our be-
" loved fovereign Don Ferdinand the fixth
" had their indifpenfible term, and his no-
" torious virtues obtained their everlafting
" reward. After having made a proper ufe
" of a happy interval of eafe which the di-
" vine clemency granted him, this moft pi-
" ous monarch died in the arms, and affifted
" with the fpiritual attendance of the arch-
" bifhop inquifitor-general, of the bifhop
" of Palencia, of the palace curate Don
" Jofeph

"Joseph de Rada, and of Don Francisco
"de Barcena, chaplain of honor to his majesty
"in the palace of Villaviciosa belonging to
"the most serene infant duke of Parma his
"brother, as count of Chinchon. He con-
"fessed himself much to the satisfaction of
"the before-mentioned Don Joseph de Ra-
"da, who administered that sacrament to
"him, and when nearer his death that of
"the extreme unction, as did the archbi-
"shop of Laodicea, nuncio to his holiness,
"the absolution and papal benediction the
"evening of his majesty's failing. He died
"at forty-five years of age, ten months and
"nine days, after a reign of thirteen years,
"one month and a day, and the same day
"in which he was proclaimed in the year
"1746. The tears shed by his vassals for
"his painful and long infirmity will make
"the best eulogium of our deceased sovereign,
"as well as their vows and prayers, with
"which they have incessantly supplicated
"his re-establishment of heaven, as also the
"patience

" patience with which they have borne the
" fufpenfion of near a year in government,
" without the leaft diforder or inquietude,
" and with a refpect and love of juftice only
" to be hoped for from the fidelity of this
" nation. His reign will be rendered equally
" glorious by the eafe and tranquillity, which
" his people have enjoyed during the courfe
" of it (to the no fmall praife of his truly
" pious heart, fince having inherited the
" crown in war, he refted not till he poffef-
" fed it in peace), as alfo by fo wife a con-
" duct, that neither the hazards, in which the
" cruel perturbations fuffered by the neigh-
" bouring powers with whom Spain is moft
" connected in intereft, threw him, nor the
" flattering confiderations which might have
" offered, made him in the leaft fwerve from
" his maxim, that peace is the greateft good to
" a nation, and that the monarch really glo-
" rious is he who procures it, taking care at
" the fame time with worthy interior provi-

" dence that his vassals do not abuse the ad-
" vantages which attend repose.

" Immediately after the death of our so-
" vereign Don Ferdinand the sixth, couriers
" were dispatched with the news of it, not
" less important than melancholy, to our
" present sovereign Don Carlos the third,
" king of the two Sicilies, and to the queen
" mother, sovereign regent of these king-
" doms, till the arrival of her son, as well
" by anticipated powers from his Sicilian
" majesty, as by the last disposition of the
" deceased king, and also, if there were oc-
" casion, by the general acclamation of those
" who cannot forget the part she acted in
" the glorious reign of our late king Don
" Philip the fifth her royal consort. O hap-
" py nation! for whom the Omnipotent in
" depriving them of so glorious a master,
" had prepared the consolation of another
" not less illustrious, nor less a lover of his
" country, and even of greater experience
" in

" in the arts of government (a good fortune
" to which monarchies are not accuftomed)
" and during his abfence, of the regent
" moft capable of fupplying his place in the
" direction of affairs, and who, as his mo-
" ther, is beft adapted to alleviate that anxi-
" ety, with which it is natural his vaffals
" fhould defire the fight of their fove-
" reign."

Seville, 20th Auguft. This evening I leave Seville, and reckon to be at Port St. Mary's to-morrow morning early, as I go by *Diligenzia*, to ufe a Spanifh expreffion, that is, I pay fomething extraordinary to travel all night, and a pretty good trot, otherwife I fhould have gone only a foot pace, and been, perhaps, two days upon the road. One of the great advantages of going in this manner is the travelling all by night, except, indeed, a little in the evening and morning, by which means you avoid being broiled alive in the very violent

fun

fun of these countries. They have no post horses in the southern parts of Spain, but for couriers on horse-back. My next paper then will, probably, be directed to you from Port St. Mary's.

LETTER LII.

PORT ST. MARY'S, AUG. 22, 1759.

UPON my arrival at this place I have found great news, which I think I cannot pleafe you better than by fending you.

Extract of a letter from Gibraltar, without a date.

" The Gibraltar frigate appeared off this
" port the 16th inftant, firing guns and
" making falfe fires. This happened after
" feven in the evening. Some time after
" fhe came into the bay to fpeak with
" admiral Bofcawen, who being informed
" by the captain that a fleet was off Ceuta
" Point, confifting of fifteen fail, ordered
" all his fhips to flip and chafe, which they
" performed with fuch furprifing celerity,
" that

"that by ten they were all under way,
"tho' not a sail was bent before, which it
"must be owned was unlucky. Since their
"departure the only intelligence we have
"received is what you sent express. It
"afforded universal joy here, as every body
"imagines Boscawen has fallen in with the
"seven ships that separated, and had not at
"the time you wrote joined those arrived in
"the bay of Bulls. My cousin lay on
"board the Intrepid that night, and as I
"have not seen or heard of him since, I
"suppose he chose to embrace an opportu-
"nity that he never, perhaps, could see
"again, of being an ocular witness of Bri-
"tish bravery. I hope soon to congratulate
"you upon our success, and to advise you
"in my next that this bay is decorated with
"seven French men of war."

Extract of a letter from Cadiz without a date, which I have translated from the Spanish.

"We

"We have the pleasure of reading in the journal or naval diary of a Spanish ship just arrived into the bay; that admiral Boscawen came up with M. la Clue's squadron at one o'clock in the day time on the 17th instant, fifteen leagues to the south of Cape St. Mary's. That the firing began at the same hour, and continued till seven at night, when the Spanish captain lost sight of them. He says the fire was most terrible; that there was one ship entirely dismasted, and many others very badly treated; that he knew of nothing more, having lost sight of them at the before mentioned time; however, we may collect from hence that the French have been all taken or destroyed. I will give you more particulars in the evening, when the Spanish ship will be quite come into port. Compliments to the consul, &c.

Extract

Extract of a letter from the same gentleman.

"Cadiz, August 22, 1759. This moment are arrived in a Portuguese boat two French officers belonging to the squadron which was commanded by M. la Clue, one of whom is wounded. They give a full account of the late battle of the seventeenth, in which the French admiral and rear admiral's ships were burnt, three of seventy guns taken, and they imagine the two others have escaped. In the evening I will write what else occurs, &c.

"P. S. The English ships suffered but little."

An English gentlemen here has just heard from a French captain, that Boscawen has blown up two ships, sunk two, and that two

two others have run themselves on shore on the coast of Spain, and one escaped.

This is all I have been able to collect you of these good news, which have rejoiced us very much, and made the remaining part of la Clue's squadron now in the bay of Cadiz look very dejected. There are three ships of the line and five frigates. In all likelihood their departure from hence will not be very soon, as our fleet will keep a good watch over them, and till the coast is clear I dare say they will not venture out.

——We do not know whether la Clue is alive or dead.

I must now tell you an escape I think I had in my journey from Seville to this place. You know we were to travel all night, and in the middle of it my servant and I were trotting quietly on in the calache, or two wheeled chaise, through a wide extended flat,

flat, said to be overflowed by the Guadalquivir or Betis during the winter season. The postilion had a dog who ran by the side of the mules, who all on a sudden began to bark, tho' we saw no object to excite his attention. We grasped, however, our pistols, and shortly after three men rose from off the ground, on which they had been lying prostrate in dark coloured jackets, hardly distinguishable from the earth itself. Two came to the right hand side of the chaise, where I was sitting, and one to the left; for though my servant declares he saw four, and the postilion five, I distinguished no more than I mention. They let us, however, pass, which I attribute to their seeing the pistols; for tho' it was night, I dare say the bright gleam of English steel might have struck their eyes. Be it as it may, the chaise passed unmolested, but no sooner were we gone by than they began running after us. The postilion, who must be an honest fellow, put his mules upon a gallop.

gallop. I held a piſtol out at the window behind, which there is in moſt foreign carriages, but, tho' both my ſervant and the poſtilion urged me to fire, I reſolved not to do it till one of the aſſailants touched the chaiſe, that I might make ſure of him. After running, however, perhaps a hundred yards, they ſtopped, and we heard no more of them.

LETTER LIII.

PORT ST. MARY'S, AUG. 31, 1759.

I Will now give you the beſt account I can of the affair between the French fleet from Toulon and that under admiral Boſcawen. I had it from the vice conſul of Cadiz, who being at Gibraltar at the time of the fleet's ſetting ſail from thence, out of curioſity went with them on board the Intrepid, to be an ocular witneſs of Engliſh bravery.

The French fleet, conſiſting of ten ſhips of the line and five frigates, ſailed out of Toulon with an intention, as ſome imagine, of going to Breſt and eſcaping, if poſſible, Boſcawen at Gibraltar. People differ, however, very much in their opinions about their deſtination. I have heard that the French themſelves profeſs to have been going to
Marti-

Martinico. I wonder indeed they make so much a secret of an expedition, which as it seems entirely frustrated, the concealing it can hardly now be of any service. But wherever they were bound, they arrived at the streights of Gibraltar the sixteenth of this month, and lay to till towards night, when they intended to pass through the *Gut*. The night was very dark, and I suppose they had chosen purposely for passing the streights a time when there was no moon. About an hour after sun-set they arrived at Ceuta point. The Gibraltar frigate, who was then cruising in the streights, perceived them, and immediately directed her course to Gibraltar bay, upon her entering which, she began firing guns and making false fires without end. I need not tell you false fires are a sort of rockets, intended for giving signals, and which they whirl about in their hands. Boscawen at last perceived her. He was then on board the Namur, but had dined in Spain that day, and if I mistake not with Bucareli the commander of the Spanish camp near Gibraltar, for the Spaniards have formed lines there, and keep a constant guard upon us. But wherever he dined, with Bucareli or the Commissioner *, he was certainly on board before the Gibraltar made her signals, tho' calumny has said the contrary. Indeed I hear he always sleeps on board, and obliges all the captains to do the same, in short, keeps a very good and strict discipline throughout the whole fleet. Upon the Gibraltar's signals he immediately ordered the fleet to sail. Surprising, says the gentleman I had this account from, was the haste with which every thing was got ready. Tho' three ships had their sails unbent, that is not put up to the yards, yet in two hours time they were all out of port and upon their way, for it was towards eight o'clock when the Gibraltar made her signals, and by ten they were at sea. Boscawen's and some other ships were out even before, but the whole fleet was under sail by that time. A Spaniard

---

* He dined with the Commissioner.

niard who was at Gibraltar compared the confusion of the town to a hell upon earth. Nor were the land officers wanting in their jokes upon the English navy in having let the French fleet slip by. The French too, who had now passed the Gut, and thought themselves secure from being attacked, were shewing their wit at our expence, as was known afterwards. In one of the ships they drew a figure of admiral Boscawen standing upon the top of the hill at Gibraltar, with a great pair of spectacles upon a nose which reached quite over to Ape's-hill, the ancient mount Abila in Barbary, while the French were sailing under it. That division too of their fleet which came in here, as they did not imagine their companions were so closely pursued, were not without their sneers. *Ma foi,* says one of them to an Englishman, alluding to poor Byng's affair, *il faut pendre Mr. Boscawen,* with many other things of this nature. In the mean time Boscawen in the Namur led the way to the reſt of the fleet, following however the Gibraltar frigate, who the moment ſhe had perceived her ſignals were underſtood at Gibraltar, had hung out all her lights, and followed the track of the ſhips ſhe had ſeen paſs by, always keeping Boſcawen in ſight, who had hung out all his lights too, and kept following her as the reſt of the fleet did him. In this poſition ſtood the chaſe all that night. It blew freſh, which you know is a ſailor's expreſſion for a ſtorm. My friend, who was on board the Intrepid, ſays not a word was to be heard on board their ſhip, except from time to time the quarter maſter ſinging out the word " ſteady," which is the term uſed by our mariners, when the ſhip goes before the wind.

Indeed I muſt take this opportunity of making an excuſe for entering into the deſcription of an affair, which I am by no means capable

capable of painting properly, from my being entirely ignorant of sea phrases. But as I am no sailor, any blunder of that kind will be excusable.

LETTER LIV.

PORT ST. MARY's, AUGUST 29, 1759.

THE chafe after the French fleet continued all night in the manner I have defcribed it to you in my laſt paper, and in the morning feven ſhips were difcovered as far off as they could fee. Tho' feven feemed too fmall a number for a French fleet, and tho' it was very probable they might belong to that of the Spaniards now in Cadiz, yet we continued chafing with all the fail poffible. The captain of the Shannon frigate, who is now at Cadiz, fays, for his part, he thought he and his crew fhould have been all ſtarved, for he was going to lay up to be cleaned at Gibraltar when the French paffed, and letting fail fo unexpectedly, he had only five days provifion on board. If the chafe had continued for fome days nobody, undoubtedly,

edly, would have ſtopt to victual his ſhip, and he and his crew muſt have made the beſt ſhift they could. Indeed he might have left the chaſe and gone into ſome port, but every perſon had too much ardor to do that, and the whole fleet ſeemed inſpired by one ſoul to get on as faſt as they could. The firſt were the Namur, the Swiftſure, the Warſpite, the Culloden, the America, the Newark, and the Intrepid. They got up with the French at one o'clock in the afternoon. They had known them to be ſuch a good many hours before, by the things they had thrown out of their ſhips. You know all ſhips are obliged to clear away their lumber before an engagement. The French threw out a prodigious number of things. Fine pieces of carved furniture were ſeen floating about the ſea. " G—d d—n " them," ſays a ſailor on board the Intrepid, " thoſe ſhips are French, I know them by " their fine guts." No perſon any longer doubting who they were, every art was put in
practice

practice to get up with them, which, as I before told you, they did at one o'clock in the afternoon. It was certainly very surprising how the English fleet could come up with the French so soon, for the French vessels in general are reckoned better sailers, and they were just come out of port, whereas ours were very foul. Now to come up with them at one o'clock when they were only just visible in the morning, is most amazing, nor is there any way of accounting * for it but from the French fleet's separation, and thinking us their companions, which was certainly a lucky thing. The cause of this division seems to be but very lamely explained by the French, and in very different manners, a sort of proof that none of them are true. Some say that in the night time in coming, out of the streights, the part of the squadron which entered Cadiz heard a couple of guns

* Our English officers attribute it entirely to the wind, which they say blew fresh near the shore, but had died away farther out at sea.

which

which was their admiral's fignal for flackening fail, but which came from the Englifh fleet, fo that they confounded one with the other, and towards the morning, finding themfelves alone, they put into Cadiz. Others fay that a ftorm feparated them juft as they came out of the *Gut*, and that opening their fealed orders to be confulted on fuch an occafion, they found that, in cafe of feparation near the ftreights, they were to go to Cadiz, which they accordingly did. But in whatever manner they divided, it could hardly be voluntary, for never was a fleet fplit in that manner, and all the great and beft fhips with the admirals and other chief officers in one divifion, and in the other all the frigates, and the three fmalleft fhips of the line, with only a chance commander. But this is what the French muft explain if they can. Now we imagine that La Clue and his feven great fhips, when he faw us, thought us to be the reft of his fquadron, and flackened fail for us to get up with him. What renders this

more

more likely is, that the seven before-mentioned ships of Boscawen were the only ones that were in sight for a long time, so that the French might easily imagine it was the remainder of their fleet with one ship wanting by some accident or other, for the division at Cadiz consists of eight, three vessels of the line and five frigates, as I have told you. La Clue, however, when he perceived his error began to prepare for the engagement with all the speed he could, sailing on, while he prepared, as fast as his ships would go, in hopes still of getting away from us, but it was then too late, as the high wind which blew assisted our heavy ships, and enabled them to keep on steadier and carry more sail, with other advantages enjoyed by us in a greater degree than by the French. Our fleet being at length come up, hostilities began, of which it would be dull to give you the very minute account my friend did me. However in my next paper I will tell you some of the principal circumstances, for

to

to say the truth, I heard so much about the engagement, and people asked him so many questions at a time, that every thing is quite confused in my head.

LET-

LETTER LV.

PORT ST. MARY'S, SEPT. 2, 1759.

WHILE the remains of our fleet came lagging behind, Boscawen's ship the Namur attacked the Ocean, which was that of the French admiral. It is said he would have taken her that evening, but an unlucky shot brought his fore or mizen mast, I do not know which, by the board. Immediately the French gave three shouts, and made the air ring again with *vive le roy*. Boscawen finding his ship rendered unfit for command, took down his flag, got into his barge, and went on board the Newark, which stood next him. The sea was still *roughish*, notwithstanding the firing of the cannon in an engagement generally lays the waves. The English greatly complain against the French for aiming at the admiral like a bird, as he passed

passed from one ship to the other, which it seems is contrary to the rules of war. But Boscawen was soon on board the Newark, where he hoisted his flag, and the battle went on as brisk as ever. At last, night approached and favoured the French, who seemed to have no other idea than that of sailing off as fast as they could. Nay, even when the Ocean dismasted the Namur, after the three cheers away she went, but was intercepted by some others of our ships. And now under favor of the night they all crouded as much sail as possible and drove on before the wind. We followed them as well as the great darkness of the weather would permit. The Centaur, indeed, had struck the evening before, but still there remained six others. In the morning, however, four only were to be seen anchored under the coast of Portugal, which they had made in the night. The two others, which were the Guerrier and Sovereign, had disappeared, nor to this day is there any certain account what has become of them. They may have got to Lisbon * the nearest port, and we not have heard of it yet, but many, nay even the French themselves, are apt to think they went to the bottom, as they certainly were much shattered in the engagement. Admiral Boscawen, however, has sent two ships after them, which, if they are to be found, will, I dare say, give a good account of them. But to return to the four French ships at anchor. Finding themselves freshly attacked by Boscawen, the Modéste and Temeraire after a small resistance struck, but the Ocean and Redoubtable cut away their anchors and run on shore. " Look what " cowardly d—gs they are," says one of the sailors, who saw the Ocean driving on shore, and he had hardly pronounced the words, when she struck against the ground, the

* After a tedious voyage they at last got into La Rochelle in France.

shock

shock of which brought every one of her masts by the board. The greatest part of the officers and sailors, as well of the Ocean as the Redoubtable, by getting into their boats and rowing briskly escaped being made prisoners. I think, however, we took out about one hundred and fifty, the greatest part of them wounded, when we went on board the Ocean to set fire to her, which same fate was shared by the Redoubtable, and they say when the latter blew up she made a most terrible explosion. She shook the very sea under all our ships. The powder on board the Ocean had got wet, as she had bulged in striking upon the shore. In this vessel there were two or three millions of livres (at least so it is reported) which in the hurry and confusion were not found. The sailors, however, got some long ruffled shirts, which they afterwards put on and looked very ridiculous. During the small resistance these ships made in the morning, a little Portuguese fort near which the combatants then

were,

were, fired upon both, to shew them, I suppose, that they were under the king of Portugal's protection, but whether by chance or purposely, a broadside from one of our ships laid it flat to the ground. These are the principal circumstances I have been able to collect concerning this action, some parts of which the French, who have sought refuge at Cadiz, set in a very different light. They say the English burnt the one hundred and fifty men alive in the Ocean, that the whole fleet came up with their ships and that they made a most astonishing resistance. " Did " not such a man," says a passionate Frenchman, who was exposing himself in a coffeehouse at Cadiz, " did not he continue fight-" ing to the last, tho' he had an arm shot " off? Such another, did not he do the same " without any legs?" I do not know whether he did not say a man came upon deck and fought without a head. However the English agree that monsieur de Chabranc, captain of the Centaur, who is now at Gibraltar,

raltar, behaved with the moſt remarkable bravery; but if we are to believe the French every common man was equal to a captain, and the captains themſelves ſomething more than mortal.

LETTER LVI.

PORT ST. MARY'S, SEPT. 5, 1759.

ADMIRAL Bofcawen's victory over the feven fhips being now compleat, having taken or deftroyed all of them except the two which I have already informed you difappeared in the night time, feparated his fleet into two divifions, his and that of Admiral Broderick, and went in queft of the remainder of the French fleet; I mean the eight fhips which put into Cadiz, not the two which efcaped by favor of the night. The exact number of them he did not know, nor where they were gone, but that there were more belonging to the feven he had to do with was undoubted. As for the two that efcaped in the night, the Sovereign and Guerrier, two veffels were, as I faid, difpatched after them, which, if I miftake not,

fteered

steered towards Lisbon; and we have a current report here of the former being taken. It is reckoned a very particular circumstance that those ships should get so entirely out of sight as not to have the least glimpse of them visible in the morning. And it is this makes some people imagine that one, if not both, may have gone to the bottom, and to strengthen this idea, my friend says, that the night after the engagement, while they were chasing the four ships, single guns like those of distress were heard at a distance. But time will inform us of the truth of every thing. The French who escaped in their boats from the Ocean and Redoubtable, and were about two thousand, got to Lagos, the nearest little town upon the coast of Portugal. They give a dismal account of this place, and of the terrible situation of Mr. la Clue there, wounded, and without any of the conveniences a man in his condition requires. They say that one day two louis d'ors were given to buy a patridge to

make him some broth. The French complain, likewise, greatly against the Portuguese for denying common coarse provisions to the sailors, but I think the excuse the latter give is very satisfactory, that they have it not. Indeed, an English gentleman, who has been there, says he could hardly find victuals in Lagos for himself and his companion, much less can it be done for two thousand people. However, I believe the greatest part of them are now come to Cadiz, at least, of those who are not wounded. I myself saw two open boats of them come in, for those were the best conveyances they could get, who but a few days before were masters of the Ocean and Redoubtable. Some of the poor fellows were most miserably dreſt, nor did any thing of finery remain to hardly any of them, except the hat and feather, the all in all of a French officer. Some of the wounded when they are well enough to change place, are, they say, to be quartered here at Port St. Mary's, in a sort of hospita-
hired

hired for that purpofe. Many of thofe that are well are already fet out for Malaga, where they hope to find an embarkation for France, if not, to go by land to Barcelona. As for La Clue, we are not only uncertain where he is at prefent, but in what manner he is wounded. We were firft of all told that both his legs were carried off—we then funk it to one, and now they fay he has loft neither, but that he has them very much *fracaffées*, with the calf of one gone. It is reported they have carried him from Lagos to St. Lucar, and that they intend to bring him here as foon as poffible. I need not tell you that Admiral Bofcawen was fcratched with fplinters all about his face and body without any dangerous wound, for I believe he may be in England before my letter, as there is a frefh report that he is gone there with his divifion, but how true I know not; for one moment the people fay one thing, and the next they contradict it. I fhould imagine, however, that upon hearing the remainder of the French fleet is in Cadiz harbour, he will send some of his ships to watch them. He has dispatched the Edgar, the Centaur prize, and two or three other ships that were in the battle to Gibraltar. The Temeraire and Modeste, which were taken, are said to be so little damaged, that they are cruising with Broderick.

Tho' the Frenchmen, with which Cadiz now swarms, are crest-fallen, yet at the same time they are very impertinent. In their turn, however, they suffer many insults from the common Spaniards, who you know hate them, tho' the government of late years has been in the hands of the Bourbon family. Coming in a public boat the other day from Cadiz to Port St. Mary's, as we were going along side a French vessel, the boatman hollowed out in broken English, " how do you do, sirs?" and I hear it is a common practice with the watermen to teaze them

them in this manner. Indeed, they deserve it, for the young officers are most unsufferable. They will have an opportunity, however, of cooling their blood in the port of Cadiz, for I do not believe they will move from thence till the war is over. The Spaniards in joke advise them to sell their ships to the king of Spain. They wanted to go out the other day under convoy of Navarro's fleet, the Spanish admiral, who is gone to Naples to fetch the new king or queen of Spain, or both. It was, as you may imagine, refused them. They next desired him to take at least some of their men on board, and set them down in the nearest port they could to France, but that was not granted neither. I flatter myself that we shall now experience the Spaniards better friends than they have been for some years.

LETTER LVII.

PORT ST. MARY'S, SEPT. 9, 1759.

I Have now finished my account of the affair between Boscawen and La Clue. The loss of the English is I think only one hundred and thirty-five men killed, among which are but two or three officers. That of the French must have been much more considerable, but as they either do not know, or at least do not care to tell it, there can be no certainty. The French in the mean time refugeed at Cadiz have rendered themselves much disliked by all parties, by their vaunting behaviour, not to be smothered under adversity. The Roman catholic Irish declare that tho' the government of England is the object of their detestation, they would sooner have us for masters than this overbearing people. Their opinion, however, with regard

gard to the Spaniards seems quite different, and they think in case of a Spanish descent in Ireland, that they would be assisted by all the Roman-catholics, which you know are numerous.

And now to say a word about Port St. Mary's and Cadiz, two towns situated upon different sides of a large bay, but the intercourse between which is rendered very easy by the boats continually going backwards and forwards. They have been both taken by the English. Cadiz in queen Elizabeth's reign by Sir Francis Drake and the earl of Essex; and Port St. Mary's in the year 1702 under Sir George Rooke and the duke of Ormond, assisted by the Dutch. Cadiz was at that time attempted by the united fleets of England and Holland; but as they were able to do nothing against that town, they threw themselves upon the other side of the bay. The Spanish government of Port St. Mary's upon being summoned to surrender, only
returned

returned this sullen answer, " that Castil-
" lians never change their king or their reli-
" gion." The present deplorable condition
of this once opulent and populous city is attributed to the English invasion, since which
time it has been almost abandoned as inse-
cure. Even grass is growing in some of the
streets, and several fine palaces are altogether
uninhabited and run to decay. However, it
is a more agreeable town to me than Cadiz,
which the hurry and confusion of so many
people, who are sacrificing their ease for interest, renders a very unpleasing sojourn to a
student.

. I shall set out next week for Gibraltar,
which is about two day's journey from
hence. It is not absolutely impossible but I
may there embark with our ambassador to
the emperor of Marocco, appointed for re-
deeming the slaves taken upon the loss of the
Litchfield. Some things, however, may
arise to hinder me from putting this design
into execution. LET-

LETTER LVIII.

GIBRALTAR, SEPT. 24, 1759.

As you will see by my date I am at length in the British garrison. You shall now have a description of what little happened worth relating in my journey hither.

Dinner over at Port St. Mary's I put myself into a little row-boat which was to conduct me to Cadiz. Due ceremonies finished with the custom-house officers, who are rather troublesome in these parts, our diminutive vessel bore us out of the river Guadalete near the mouth of which Port St. Mary's is situated, and we entered into that vast bay, which takes its denomination from the town of Cadiz, the principal of the many that are dispersed round it. It may be two or three English leagues from Port St. Mary's

Mary's to Cadiz, but patience and four oars at laſt brought us among the ſhips, moſt of which are anchored near the walls of the city. The firſt we came to was a Britiſh veſſel, the Princeſs Louiſa, whoſe waving colours ſeemed to bid defiance to a couple of the French frigates that lay near her. A little farther on was the Shannon frigate, with whom I had intended to come to Gibraltar, but her loitering ſo long at Cadiz made me at laſt reſolve to travel by land. She ſtays, I think, for money to be brought hither, but if that is the caſe her delay may be long, as the queen dowager and regent has forbidden the exportation of any of that vaſt quantity of bullion arrived lately at Cadiz in the Spaniſh fleet from the Weſt Indies. I wonder that Spain and Portugal, the only European nations who have mines of any great value, ſhould not conceive that gold is as much a commodity with them as cloth with us. If they hinder us from receiving the product of their countries, how can they

expect

expect we should give them those of ours? A Portuguese nobleman was complaining to lord Tyrawley, when ambassador at Lisbon, how hard it was that such prodigious sums of their money should go annually into England. He replied that nothing was more easy in the world than for the Portuguese to remedy that complaint. Upon being asked in what manner, with an eagerness that shewed how agreeable such a piece of instruction would be, he answered dryly, "that all they "had to do was neither to eat nor cloath them- "selves." This, he said, alluding to the great quantities of corn and cloth yearly exported from England to that kingdom. Indeed of late the produce of our lands has been so little that we have been obliged to prohibit the exportation of wheat, and the Portuguese to seek for it elsewhere, but at present I hope from two years tolerable crops with us, things will be reinstated in their usual channel. Now for a nation, who has not bread to eat, nor cloth to cloath themselves with, to be unwilling to purchase it with their very unuseful commodity in itself, gold, is a folly of which I flatter myself few people with us would be capable. This same maxim of keeping their gold in their country holds as good in Spain as in Portugal, tho' there is not so great a balance of trade in our favour, for many more commodities come to us from Spain than Portugal, which latter, excepting its fruit and wines does not, I believe, send the value of a shilling in goods to England, whereas it is said we cannot make our superfine cloth without the help of Segovia wool. But the queen dowager of Spain, intoxicated with the idea of enriching her kingdom and making it overflow with gold, has prohibited the exportation of money, at least of that which arrived lately to Cadiz, and which is not allowed as yet to be given out to its particular owners. As for any other it may, I believe, be exported at a certain duty per cent. which I do not think is an unfair way. But what I am

afraid

afraid of is, that England, without being allowed to take fome of this money, will not get enough to repay the two millions of dollars (a dollar is about three and fix-pence) that are due to her. Nay, it is thought it will be hard to get what little our garrifon here wants, and our Marocco ambaffador in particular, in order to redeem the three hundred flaves now in that kingdom, the remains of the crew that belonged to the Litchfield, &c. It will coft about forty thoufand pounds to ranfom them.

LETTER LIX.

GIBRALTAR, SEPT. 27, 1759.

I Left you in my laſt paper in the middle of the bay of Cadiz, gazing at the different ſhips anchored there, which raiſed a diſſertation upon money. I will now land you upon the mole, which is adorned with two large columns, that mean to repreſent the pillars of Hercules, in commemoration of thoſe which he is ſaid to have erected in theſe parts (tho' properly at Gibraltar or the ancient Calpe,) as being arrived to the end of the world; for in ſuch light did the ancients conſider the weſtern parts of Europe, as they were ignorant of America. The *ne plus ultra* written upon theſe fabulous columns is not badly alluded to in the large Spaniſh ſilver coins, by a ſhip's ſailing through them with the words *plus ultra* inſcribed. Upon my
entrance

entrance into the town, I met the person I wanted, who is a merchant of Gibraltar, and who was to accompany me hither. I had got acquainted with him at Port St. Mary's, where he came to see the new king proclaimed, a ceremony consisting of nothing but a cavalcade round the town, which stopped in the different squares, while marquis Terri, with the royal standard in his hand, mounted scaffolds erected for that purpose, and pronounced the following words; beginning with an *oyes*, which is literally Spanish for *hear*.

" Oyes, oyes, oyes,

" Castille, Castille, Castille, and the great
" port of St. Mary's. Long live our sove-
" reign lord Don Carlos the third."

These words were no sooner out of his mouth than about a hundred pieces of silver scattered among the mob set them to scrambling and crying out *viva* with all
their

their might. We hear that the Auſtrian ambaſſador at Madrid has objected to the title of Charles the third being given to the preſent king, and has declared, by order from his court, that he ought to be called Charles the fourth, upon account of the emperor Charles the ſixth, then archduke of Auſtria, having ruled in Spain for ſome little time, before the more fortunate arms of Philip the fifth expelled him from that kingdom. But the caſe is, that he never was publicly proclaimed or acknowledged, and therefore does not enter properly into the liſt of Spaniſh kings.

At Cadiz we were much diſtreſſed by not being able to find horſes to carry us to Gibraltar, as the governor of that town had laid an embargo upon them to attend the French, who once belonged to the Ocean and Redoubtable, to Malaga, where they were in hopes of finding ſome conveyance to return to France. Indeed, I think it was

doing

doing their nation much honor to employ all the hireable horſes of a populous city, to convey their perſons to the deſired port; but the governor of Cadiz is eſteemed a thorough well wiſher to their cauſe, and all his actions have ſufficiently teſtified it, and in particular the affair of the Antigallican privateer, which tho' our court ſeems to lie dormant at preſent, will not, I believe, be ſo eaſily forgotten. You, perhaps, know the affair as well as I, but in a few words it was this. The Antigallican privateer, tho' of inferior force, took upon the coaſt of Gallicia the duke de Penthievre, a rich French Eaſt-Indian veſſel. The people on board her confeſſed themſelves legally captured. The Antigallican carried her into Cadiz. By ſubornation, as it is ſaid, the governor got ſome of the French priſoners to ſwear the contrary in that port, to what they had affirmed at ſea. They ſwore the duke de Penthievre when taken was within cannon ſhot of a Spaniſh fort. The affair came to a trial, a trial, which was given against Foster, the captain of the Antigallican, and his prize was not only wrested from him, but his own ship taken away by force and given to the French, who are now fitting her out, and I believe she is to sail as soon as ever admiral Broderick's fleet, who are now off Cadiz, will permit her. The affair has been, I believe, transmitted to Madrid by appeal, but I know not that any answer has been obtained. As for the governor of Cadiz, I believe he now begins to retract a little, since the accession of the new king to the throne, and the great success of the English. Now fortune smiles, we begin to find all people our friends. At the time of the loss of Port Mahon, when Great Britain was taking a nap, as the world thought we were down, each was giving a shove to push us lower. It is the way of the world.

LETTER LX.

GIBRALTAR, OCTOBER 1, 1759.

THE disappointment of not finding horses made us resolve to take a boat, and go over to Chiclana, which was in our way, in hopes of finding some there. Chiclana is about twelve miles from Cadiz, at the very end of the bay, two or three miles up the country, upon a little river that conveys boats to it. But we had not gone half the way, when certain black clouds arose to the levant or east, which would not permit us to stir a step further in the course we were sailing. There was, likewise, some thunder, and we expected rain, but we had not any till two or three days ago, which has finely refreshed the air, and it is now the most pleasant weather that can be imagined.

If we could compound the two climates of Spain and England by remitting them some of our rain, and receiving in return a little dry weather, they would both be the finest in the world. However, at present I cannot but think that we are rather too wet at home, and that the beholding something more of the sun would not do us any harm. But yet the prodigious blaze he shines forth with here in Spain, while he rides so near us for months together without one cloud or drop of rain to cool the air, seems to me an excess on the contrary side.

The thunder and contrary wind hindering us from being able to put into execution our intended expedition by water to Chiclana; we were obliged to take the boatman's advice, and stop short at a place called La Isla, or the island, tho' only separated, as well as Cadiz, from the main land by a small stream, over which there is a bridge. We here got horses, and proceeded upon our journey

journey to Chiclana about half an hour before sun-set. We went upon a good made road, like a turnpike in England, for about three miles, through a country where there were nothing but salt-pits. The manner they make salt in these hot dry climates is by letting the sea into holes dug for that purpose, where the force of the sun dries it up, and the sediment that remains is salt. The latter part of our road was through a sort of forest, and but indifferent. The muskatoes were, likewise, very troublesome, and hung as thick as they could cluster upon the boughs of the trees. At last, tho' some time after dark, we arrived at Chiclana, and put up at a French inn there. Our landlord welcomed us to the *hotel* as he termed it; for Chiclana being a pretty place, many of the French, who swarm at Cadiz, make excursions to it from thence for the benefit of a little fresher air, which makes it worth while to keep a better and consequently more expensive house. We here with difficulty got horses and a guide, and set out in the morning before it was light for Gibraltar.———

LETTER LXI.

GIBRALTAR, OCTOBER 4, 1759.

THE rising sun gave us a view of our cattle, which were not of the most excellent kind. It was now, however, too late to complain, and we comforted ourselves that the present road was very good, tho' we had the mortification of knowing that which was to come to be most villainous, nay, they even went so far as to say that it was almost impassible. We dined in a miserable inn at a place called Vexel, situated upon the top of a mountain, which we ascended by mistake, as we ought to have baited in the bottom. The way down again was most rugged and bad, and we were obliged to walk it, and stay in a most wretched hovel in the valley, till our horses could be got to us. Poor as this habitation was, we found some

excellent

excellent dried grapes, which I think are better than when freſh. I wonder we do not come into this way of preſerving them in England. Our grapes certainly do not ripen ſo eaſily, but that I think is no objection againſt their keeping as well. If I do not miſtake, they cloſe the end of the ſtalk, after taking care there is no rotten grape in the bunch, with ſealing-wax, and then hang them up in the air, where nothing can touch them. We intended to lie at a place called Los Varios, not above three Spaniſh leagues from Gibraltar, however, towards the evening we were glad to take up with a little hut three leagues ſhort of it. One of the principal cauſes of our falling ſo ſhort of our intentions was the very bad road, ſo bad in one rocky place, that our guide's loaded horſe could no longer ſtand upon his feet, and down he came, guide, baggage and all. The time we took in getting the poor animal up, as he had hurt himſelf, together with the debilitated ſtate of our own cattle,

made

made us determine to put up at the next houfe we fhould come to, which a countryman, I belie e the only perfon we had met all that evening, informed us was not far off. After a very flow progrefs, we at length arrived at the folitary manfion, which was a little inn in the woods for the poor people who pafs that way. You may imagine we could here get nothing, fo that we were obliged to live upon what we brought with us. As for our bedding, it confifted in a fort of broad manger built all round a room, and filled with rufhes, where we were obliged to extend our weary limbs, one lying beyond the other, but where I flept more foundly than I have done in better beds.———

LETTER LXII.

GIBRALTAR, OCTOBER 8, 1759.

WE set out from the wretched place mentioned in my last in the morning before it was light, and had luckily a good road till sun-rise. We then began entering among rocks that formed the most horribly romantic prospect I have ever, perhaps, seen in my life. The consul of Cadiz's expression concerning them will give you the best idea of the scene I was then beholding. It would make, says he, even a *buck* despair. It was a valley hemmed in by close rugged rocks, whose tops ascended to the clouds, but which were destitute of verdure, except towards the bottom, where there were a number of gloomy evergreens, tho' thinly scattered. After having passed this bad mountainous country, we came into a more

agreeable

agreeable fort of plain, tho' ſtill there was nothing particularly beautiful. And now the rock of Gibraltar began to appear in ſight. As it is of a conſiderable height, you ſee it at a conſiderable diſtance. My companion and I wiſhed each other reciprocally joy upon the view of it. It was a bright day and we could even diſtinguiſh many different parts, tho' we ſtill wanted many miles to get to our journey's end. As we were determined to arrive at St. Rock's, if poſſible, by dinner, we ſet on a good pace, leaving our guide and baggage behind. At length the whole rock of Gibraltar ſtood entirely expoſed to view. It appeared from the place where we were riding as if the ſea entirely divided it from the main land. A little on our left lay St. Rock's upon the top of a hill. This is reported to be a town built and inhabited by the Spaniards, who fled from Gibraltar upon our becoming maſters of that fortreſs. They are ſaid conſtantly with wiſhful eyes to behold their

ancient

ancient habitation, tho' few of the real inhabitants can be now living, except in their children. Upon our arrival at St. Rock's, we entered a tolerable inn, where not a bad dinner was ferved up in a room that had a moft delightful profpect. The whole garrifon of Gibraltar lay beneath us, at about the diftance of five miles, and beyond that Europa point, and beyond that the Barbary coaft; upon which the high mountain Abila, called by the Gibraltar people Ape's hill, made no inconfiderable figure. But having mentioned Barbary, it will be proper to acquaint you that I fet fail in a few days for Tetuan, with the ambaffador appointed to treat with the king of Marocco, not only for the redemption of our flaves wrecked with the Litchfield, but alfo, if poffible, to fettle a peace with thefe barbarians.

LETTER LXIII.

GIBRALTAR, OCTOBER 25, 1759.

I HAVE been obliged to omit writing to you laſt week, as a violent every-day's ague, or to uſe the apothecary's term, double tertian, rendered me incapable of applying to any thing. As this illneſs has deſtroyed my Barbary ſcheme, I ſhall ſet out in a few days for Cadiz. My journey to Tetuan proved very ſhort. On Monday the 15th I went on board the Guernſey, hurried away between the hot and cold fit of my ague, but, notwithſtanding all the buſtle that was made, we did not ſail till the morning afterwards. The wind was then a levanter, or eaſterly, which was contrary for us to lie in Tetuan bay, and our commander did not care to hazard being driven on ſhore with the

charge

charge of money we had for the redemption of the slaves. However as every thing was so far advanced, we set out in hopes of its changing the next morning. We had the Thetis frigate in company. Our voyage was very short, and, indeed, ought rather to be considered as a little cruise than any thing else, tho' we got within six or seven leagues of Tetuan that night. We lay to till morning, when finding the same wind continue we returned to Gibraltar by dinner time. Thus ended our expedition, and upon my landing I was immediately laid up with my ague. They have since had a second jaunt, but have done little more in it than in the first. Indeed all the English who had nothing to do with the ships landed, and went a shooting at Tetuan, but as for public business, I believe, there was nothing done, except sending the ambassador's secretary to the king of Marocco with the king's letter.

The ships and every thing elfe are returned, but that gentleman is still upon his courfe. I think he is to make no lefs than eight days journey of it to the place where His African majefty is at prefent He is now in an encampment among fome mountains, where he is inflicting fevere juftice upon the inhabitants, who, if I miftake not, have never been willing rightly to own his authority. This gentleman muft have but a difmal journey, with a guard of hideous Moors about him, and without any company but the king's letter, which he has got in a box. The letter is big enough for a pillow, and finely painted round the direction with flowers and I do not know what all. The words of the direction, if I can remember, are pretty nearly thefe.

" To the moft high and glorious monarch,
" the mighty and right noble Sidi Mahomet
" Ben Abdallah, emperor of the kingdoms of
" Ma-

"Marocco, Fez, Tafilet, Sus, Dahra, and the Algarve, with his other territories in Africa."

There is more of it, but I cannot recollect it. I suppose the king has written in person to the emperor, upon account of the latter being so much offended at some letters sent him signed by Mr. Pitt, for he does not understand secretaries of state. "I expect the king your master," said he, "will write to me himself," and other things of that nature.

In my next I will continue my journey to Gibraltar.

LETTER LXIV.

GIBRALTAR, OCTOBER 28, 1759.

TO finish my journey to the British garrison, we must return to where I left off, which was at our looking out at a window at St. Rock's in expectation of the appearance of dinner. But other affairs soon engrossed our attention. Gibraltar, by which I mean what the English possess, is a peninsula, and the neck of land which joins it to the rest of Spain may be a mile or more in breadth. Across this isthmus the Spaniards have run certain fortifications, which they call the lines, and they are terminated at either sea by a little fort. As there is a guard of Spanish soldiers continually here, no person can pass them without a licence first obtained from the Spanish commander, who lives at St. Rock's. The getting this licence was what was engrossing our present attention. To give you a better idea of the lines, and what I have said concerning them I will make you an extemporary sketch of them.

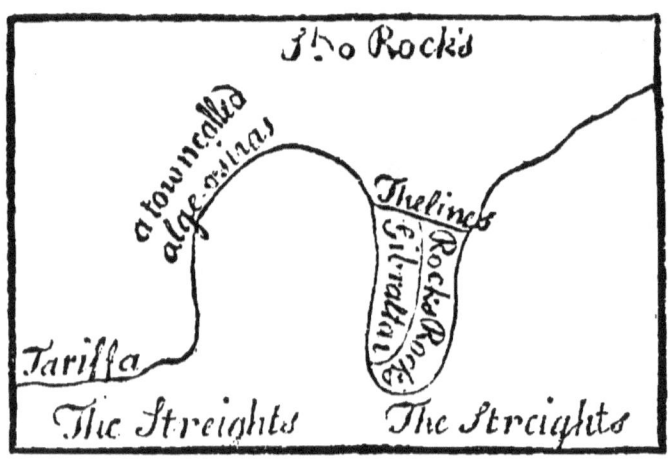

But do not think the plan I have been giving you has any pretence to perfection. Every thing is immoderately, infinitely, exorbitantly out of proportion. I only scratched it out from my own head just to give you faint idea of the position of the Spanish lines. They curb the English much.

much. When they were building, it is reported that our governor of Gibraltar at that time complained to our court about it. The ministry sent out some person, I do not know whom, to inspect the affair, and demand of the Spaniards the reason of all these hostile preparations in time of peace. The answer made was that what they were doing was with no view against the English, but for a defence against the Moors. Our good inspector was contented with the answer, and things passed off in this manner, tho' perhaps the Spaniards might think they had a right to build what they please upon their own ground. The English have since found how detrimental these lines have been, as from thence the Spaniards can annoy our ships in the bay, unless, indeed, they retire down to what is called the New Mole, which was made on that account. Finding much delay in obtaining a licence to pass this barrier, and my companion having acquaintances among the Spanish officers,

cers, we refolved to try our fortune without it. We found many English carousing with them at a hut or inn, just without the gate of the lines. In times of peace with the Spaniards, or at least at present, the English have liberty to go and dine or ride out in Spain whenever they chuse, so they have a passport from the English governor. But nobody can go fresh into the garrison from Spain without a particular licenfe from Bucareli the Spanish commander. This is the agreement the two governors have made together. Now by our mixing ourselves with the other gentlemen of the garrison, through the connivance of my companion's Spanish friends, we appeared to come under the governor of Gibraltar's permission. And in fact the centries let us pass without saying a single syllable, tho' we had afterwards much difficulty about our baggage, which we had left far behind. But other things were entertaining our thoughts at present. We were making our remarks upon the rock of Gibraltar,

raltar, which stood full before our view. We were still upon the flat deep sands that run between the two seas before you come to the town. The rock which rises perpendicularly from the ground, on the right hand of which are situated the land fortifications of the garrison, with the sea, all together formed a most romantic prospect. But we now entered the gate of Gibraltar, and I found myself once more under the protection of my native country.

LETTER LXV.

GIBRALTAR, NOV. 2, 1759.

IN my laſt paper I left you upon our entrance into Gibraltar. When we had paſt the gate and the Engliſh guard at it, our company ſeparated. My companion and I proceeded into the heart of the town, where we met ſeveral officers of his acquaintance, who recommended me to a lodging. We were now got to the parade, the beſt part of Gibraltar, and upon my word it looked very pretty, tho' perhaps it might appear better from my having come through ſo many bad towns in Spain for a foil. The next morning I paid my viſit of ceremony to the governor at the convent; for the habitation of the governors of Gibraltar was originally ſuch, and the church belonging to it is now uſed by the garriſon. When
the

the English first took this rock, which was in the year 1704, two years after the expedition to Port St. Mary's, they did not seem to know the importance of the place. It divides the two naval powers of France and Spain pretty nearly into two equal parts, and consequently, renders them both considerably weaker, as to unite their forces you see they must run the danger of passing the streights, which we have proved of late how badly it has succeeded to the French. If we had not Gibraltar, what would be easier than for the French or Spaniards to send a fleet there in time of war, and keep us entirely out of the Mediterranean? Indeed, at present we are likely to be in some degree of amity with Spain, and I hope for some time; for it does Spain and England much more reciprocal damage to be at war with each other than with France. The reason is this, that France and we, except for a few wines, and the counterband trade, have no commerce at all together. And what little

we

we have with them is prejudicial to us, as so much clear money goes out of the kingdom, for they want no products of ours in exchange. Cloth they make nearly as good as ourselves, and much cheaper. Leather, and a thousand other commodities we have in England, they want not. On the contrary, Spain takes off these and a great many more, and in return gives us a little wool, fruit, wine and oil, but the surplus is made up in good pistoles. We expect, likewise, this year to have a great deal of corn come from England into these parts, for we hear there has been a very plentiful crop with you, and in Spain, besides not an over abundance last harvest, they have not had above a shower or two these seven months. You may imagine, therefore, we have but a bad prospect for next year. Here at Gibraltar, indeed, we have had something more of rain, and one shower so prodigiously hard in the night time, that when we got up in the morning, we found the town all full of gravel, which had been washed down

from

from the hill. I have already told you, I think, that Gibraltar stands at the foot of the highest most craggy rock that can be imagined. Two very disagreeable things arise from this situation. One is, that as the mountain is pretty nearly due east, it reflects the rays of the sun in the afternoon so violently, that you feel a redoubled heat from it. The other is the ugly prospect it affords, to look upon such a blasted eminence without any thing green upon it, tho' it is said there are many botanical herbs, but they are too small to strike the eye. Indeed, the whole of Gibraltar is very contrary to a person who loves to enjoy rural scenes, but the want of green to a traveller is in great measure made up by the romanticness of the place. The most curious walk I know is down to Europa point. You go among rocks that seem rent, and torn, and displaced by millions of earthquakes, till at last you come to a sort of a point, a *ne plus ultra,* where the peninsula of Gibraltar ends.

LETTER LXVI.

CHICLANA, NOV. 5, 1759.

As you will see by my date, I am at last got thus far in my way from Gibraltar to Cadiz. Tho' I am recovered of the ague, which attacked me so violently, I may stay here a day or two, as it is reckoned fine air, in order to re-establish myself perfectly.

I have but few things to add concerning Gibraltar. The fortifications seem the most curious part of the whole place. As those towards Spain are formed and interwoven with the rock, it seems difficult, if not impossible, to dismount the guns. Willis's battery, all up in the heavens, appears to me to command what approaches the Spaniards can possibly make. The last time they besieged Gibraltar, they attempted to undermine
this

this battery, and worked on thirty yards through the living stone, but the garrison perceiving their intentions, rendered them unavailing, by blowing up the upper part of the rock as fast as they did underneath, and letting the immense stones, torn off by the force of gun-powder, roll down upon their heads. We have since overflowed the ground lying without the land-port with the sea, and have only left a cause-way, or rather bridge, to enter the town, and that is defended by what they call the grand battery, and many other cannon, particularly two which are placed by themselves, something lower than Willis's battery. They are in such a position as to command fully the entrance into the town, and by the rocks winding beside them, are difficult to be dismounted, not to mention their height. These two guns were what galled the Spaniards most in the last siege, and some even go so far as to say that they saved the place. If, however, it is any ways weak, it is towards

wards the sea, but as the ramparts are high, the landing, in case of a breach, would be dangerous; there are, however, so many guns all along that part, I do not see how a ship could lie to batter the walls without being disabled. We need not, indeed, talk of Gibraltar being attacked by sea, till we find a nation able to cope with us upon that element. All these things considered, I esteem that fortress as almost impregnable, I will not say quite, because treachery or unforeseen accidents may give the lie to the surest foresight. The back of Gibraltar is defended by nature with such inaccessible rocks, that no enemy without wings can molest us that way. The ascent to the top of them is steep towards the town, but on the other side towards the Mediterranean nearly perpendicular. On one of the highest parts of this mountain the English have erected their signal house, to give notice of the arrival of ships, as is customary

in

in ports. I went up here once out of curiofity, and once is furely enough for any perfon, fo much labour is it to get there, tho' a foldier carries up a little barrel of water every day for the ufe of the guard ftationed upon that bleak fpot. This is all his day's work, which you may think fufficient. The gentleman who accompanied me could hardly keep himfelf upon his feet, his head turned to fuch a degree, but he fays he is particularly affected that way when he comes to any precipice. He was the fecretary to our Barbary ambaffador, and who in the fecond expedition, while my ague confined me to my bed, landed and went, attended by a hundred of the emperor's guards, to Marocco, or rather to a mountain where Sidi Mahomet is encamped at prefent. Had I been well, I fhould certainly have borne him company, which he would have efteemed as no fmall favor; for he can have but unentertaining ideas in an evening, furrounded

rounded with a hundred Moorish guards, all blacks, and without any person to speak with. His errand, as I have mentioned, was to carry the king's letter.

END OF VOL. I.

www.ingramcontent.com/pod-product-compliance
Lightning Source LLC
Chambersburg PA
CBHW030551300426
44111CB00009B/944